HOLY GHOSTBUSTER

The Reverend J Aelwyn Roberts was Vicar of Llandegai in North Wales for 36 years. As Director of Social Work and Adoption Officer for the Diocese of Bangor he found himself increasingly called upon to deal with hauntings and other aspects of the paranormal. His fascinating tales about his ghost experiences have led to frequent appearances on television for BBC Wales and HTV. As well as being a consummate story-teller, he has written many stories and scripts for BBC Radio.

HOLY GHOSTBUSTER

A Parson's Encounters with the Paranormal

J. AELWYN ROBERTS

ELEMENT

Shaftesbury, Dorset ● Rockport, Massachusetts
Brisbane, Queensland

Text © J Aelwyn Roberts 1990

First published in Great Britain in 1990 by
Robert Hale Limited, London

Published in Great Britain in 1996 by
Element Books Limited
Shaftesbury, Dorset SP7 8BP

Published in the USA in 1996 by
Element Books, Inc.
PO Box 830, Rockport MA 01966

Published in Australia in 1996 by
Element Books Limited
for Jacaranda Wiley Limited
33 Park Road, Milton, Brisbane 4064

Cover design by The Pinpoint Design Company
Cover photograph of the author by Terry Fincher,
Photographers International
Typeset by Derek Doyle & Associates, Mold, Clwyd
Printed and bound in Great Britain by
J W Arrowsmith Limited, Bristol, Avon

British Library Cataloguing in Publication
data available

Library of Congress Cataloging in Publication
data available

ISBN 1–85230–913–X

Contents

Foreword 7

Acknowledgements 9

I GHOSTS AND THEIR HABITS

1 In the Beginning 13
2 Tommy 21
3 The Earthbound Ghost 26
4 Noddy 38
5 A Rustle of Ghosts 45
6 The Learner 54
7 The Renaissance 60
8 The Council House Ghost 67
9 The Smelly Ghost 76
10 The Anniversary Ghost 86
11 The Ghost That Changed House 91
12 The Last Will and Testament 99
13 The Ghost That Was Not a Ghost 103
14 The Ghost of a Living Man 107
15 The Churchyard Ghost 113
16 The Ghost of the Unmarried Mother 121
17 The Extrovert Ghost 127

II MEDIUMS AND THEIR GIFTS

1 The Gifts 137
2 Telepathy 138
3 Clairvoyance 141
4 Healing 147
5 Water-Diving – Dowsing 155
6 Cis Jones 162
7 Elwyn's Glossary 172

Foreword

The stories in this book are not fiction but accounts of some of the Rev Aelwyn Roberts' and his colleagues' experiences in ridding haunted houses of their unwelcome occupants and releasing earth-bound spirits.

Written in an easy style, sometimes with a nice sense of the ridiculous, it makes not only serious but entertaining reading.

The Lady Janet Douglas Pennant
Penrhyn
Bangor

Acknowledgements

I would like to display, in print, for all to see, my gratitude to my kind friends who have helped make the book possible.

Elwyn Roberts the research scientist, who is also so very endowed with an abundance of psychical gifts and is a most interesting companion and a loyal friend. We have had great times together.

Ray Bower, editor of *Country Quest*, who gave such encouragement at times when I was becoming quite moithered with spiritual antics.

Chloris Morgan, who introduced me to so many of her friends in the Spiritualist Church.

Winnie Marshal, who answered so many of my questions with such patience and charm and also untrapped the nerve in my heel.

Lorraine Lee, my scribe and friend, who not only typed the whole book MS for me but put up with all my whims when I changed it and chopped it and amended it. She retyped it every time without a murmur of complaint.

New friends: Members of the Spiritualist Church, freelance mediums, healers, water-diviners, dowsers, pendulum-operators, telepathy-demonstrators, clairvoyants, all of whom have helped considerably to put a rich third dimension into my life.

PART ONE

Ghosts and Their Habits

1 *In the Beginning*

There were no ghosts in the quarry village of Blaenau Ffestiniog where I grew up in the 1930s – no real ghosts. Some people said there was a *bwgan* in Coed Cwmbowydd, and others had seen a ghost on the crossroads near Manod. But these were faceless, characterless ghosts. No one who had ever seen them could remember whether they were male ghosts or female ghosts. They were just things, 'its', and the most that anyone confronted by one could remember was that they were whitish, as if they were covered in a bed sheet.

The *bwgan* and the other ghosts were things that lived outside the home on lonely crossroads or near a stile. I never knew of a single haunted house in Blaenau, but I knew of one in Betwys-y-Coed. The church choir would travel to Betws to sing in the Deanery Festival once a year. We had tea together in the church room, and afterwards we threw flat pebbles across the pools of the river before going into the church for the five o'clock rehearsal. In the trees above the river there was a large red-brick house. That house was haunted by a ghost. How we knew this I cannot tell, but we always pointed it out to each other at Deanery Festival times and said that there was a ghost there.

We had another *bwgan* in Blaenau during my growing-up time – a ghost of flesh and blood that walked through the town every night of the year at the midnight hour. The whole town knew that the little retired primary school headmistress perambulated the empty streets of the town every night. Miss Jones *Bach** had three great love-fantasies: the police superintendent, the grammar school headmaster and, strangely enough, Lord Davies of Llandinam.

* *Bach* – meaning 'little' but also used as a term of endearment.

On many a night when my college friend Dave and I took
our long after-supper walks, we would see, by the Co-op
stores, the faint flicker of candlelight. We would then step
into a dark shop entrance to allow Miss Jones *Bach* the
midnight freedom of the town. As the light flickered, we
would hear the faint humming of a beautiful little melody as
she got nearer, and then the frou-frou of her dress and her
long cloak as she passed. We would catch the faint whiff of a
most peculiar perfume – a mixture of mothballs and incense,
and then Miss Jones *Bach* would have gone. She passed so
near we could have touched her, but we would not have
dared. I wondered whether she ever knew we were there. Her
step never faltered as she walked past, swinging her lantern,
humming her little song and looking straight ahead.

We weren't frightened. There was nothing to be frightened
of, but it was always an eerie feeling as Miss Jones *Bach* went
past. Neither Dave nor I would say a word to each other until
the frail little lady had gone well on her way.

Once or twice we followed her. She would turn up into
Park Square and there pick a laurel leaf from the police
station hedge, kiss it and throw it back into the
superintendent's garden. Forward then to the grammar
school. Another laurel leaf, another kiss, another pledge of
love thrown into the headmaster's garden, and then back
home to her lonely life in her little terraced house in
Cromwell Street.

In my years of dealing with ghosts, the thrill of making
contact always reminds me of the frou-frou of Miss Jones
Bach's dress, and the smell of mothballs and incense. Had I
decided to become a teacher or a solicitor or an auctioneer, it
is quite possible that this midnight encounter with Miss Jones
Bach would have been the nearest thing to a ghost that I
would have encountered.

It is strange how we all crave for justice and equality and
parity, and yet life is not like that. It appears that in the
Kingdom of Heaven those who worked only one hour got the
same wage as those who had put in a twelve-hour shift,
bearing the heat and the burden of the day. If this happened
in the Kingdom of Earth, shop stewards all over the country
would cry, 'Everybody out! Everybody out!' But this kind of

inequality does happen in all walks of life, and shop stewards can do nothing about it.

There are in our towns and villages countless people, families even, who can boast that they have never been a patient in a hospital, nor can they recall the name of their GP of twenty years. There are others whose main topic of conversation is their first, and their second, and even their third big operation; and there are little families at whose door the undertaker's hearse seems to call practically every winter.

There are a great number of good, careful, non-drinking drivers who seem doomed to suffer a multiplicity of accidents, and there are others who enjoy their no-claims bonus for fifty years and more.

There are those in this life who enjoy the company of ghosts, and others who are troubled by ghosts, and there are millions more who go through life quite oblivious of ghosts and ghostly happenings. I merely make the point that, had I become a teacher or a solicitor or an auctioneer, I could quite easily have lived my life a ghost-unbeliever. But I became a parson, and sorting out ghostly trouble very soon became an important part of my job.

When I was eighteen, just before war broke out, I entered St David's University College and after graduating in three years entered St Michael's Theological College, Cardiff, to read theology and to be apprenticed and trained in the crafts of parish priesthood – teaching, preaching, listening, voice-production, visiting the sick, a whole gambit of arts grouped under the generic title 'Pastoralia'. But no lecturer or demonstrator uttered a single word on how to deal with ghosts.

It was a good training college, and I have often wondered why ghosts at that time were not part of the curriculum. Was it perhaps that at that particular period only celebrities, such as kings and those who died violent deaths or lived in great mansions, manifested themselves, coming back to haunt and to mystify? If this is true, there must have been a massive revolution in the great beyond in the 1950s, when all the departed demanded, and were given, the right to make frequent visits back to earth, because today the mediums I know – and who are willing to detoxify haunted houses – are being worked to the ground.

And there is also such a great interest in this occult world. Anyone starting to tell a ghost story is assured of a good audience.

Last year some world travellers took me under their wing in Turkey. We stayed in a third-rate hotel in Istanbul, and they showed me every nook and every native eating-place in that great city. The hotel in which we were staying was ten storeys high, and the lift and stairs on every floor opened out into a huge hall-cum-lounge. My friends and I were probably the only Europeans in the hotel, but it seemed very popular with the locals and a great favourite with Iranian refugees. My traveller friends and I came home to roost about midnight and before turning in to sleep had coffee in the lounge. During conversation I mentioned that I was preparing to write a book on my experiences as a ghost-hunter, and my friends John from Australia and Charlie from Alaska wanted to know more. There was a group of Iranian refugees squatting on the floor not far from us, and I could see that one of them was eavesdropping on our conversation. Presently he came over.

'You talk ghosts,' he said. 'Please may we come and listen to your talk?'

We offered them open house, and they all joined us. They sat down on their haunches facing us, like children awaiting a story. But one of them brought his chair over. Our new Iranian friend introduced him to us as 'Joe Louis', and once he had said this we all realized that this man had a terrific resemblance to the great boxer, only he seemed twice his size. He was a giant of a man. He sat on his chair quite expressionless, just listening.

I told them tale after tale of my ghostly encounters, and they seemed absolutely enthralled. I have preached to large and small congregations, and I have lectured to many clubs and societies, but never have I had a more enthusiastic audience than the refugee Iranians on the fifth-floor lounge in the hotel in Istanbul.

The leader told us that he too had seen a ghost in Britain. He asked me if I knew Topsham Road in Exeter, and I told him that I had a daughter living in Exeter and that I travelled along Topsham Road very often. He then told us that when he was a boy his father had had a house on Topsham Road, and there was one room in this house that was haunted. That room was never used; his father always kept it locked. But their family was a large one. He had many brothers and sisters, and often friends and relatives from London would ask if they could come and stay with them during the summer holidays. On these occasions his father was always tempted to reopen the haunted bedroom for the relatives.

Our new friend told us how, on one occasion, as a teenager, he had been allowed to accompany his father to open the haunted room. Father took out the key and unlocked the door, then he had pushed the door wide open. But they had not entered. Facing the door was a brass single bedstead, and as they looked into the room, the bed levitated itself a good four feet off the ground. He and his father had stared open-mouthed at this for more than a minute. Then the bed had crashed down onto the floor, and they had scampered downstairs as fast as their legs could carry them. It took hours before his father could summon sufficient courage to go upstairs again and relock the ghost bedroom.

He offered no explanation as to why a presumably British ghost chose to occupy the bedroom of a house owned by an Iranian family or, come to think of it, why good Moslem gentlemen, reincarnationists, should be displaying such an unhealthy interest in British ghosts. The narrator, however, received resounding applause from his audience, and I made a mental note to tell any future publisher of mine that, if the political climate changed, it might be worth thinking about an Iranian translation for my ghost book.

At 2 a.m. I decided it was time to go to bed. The Iranians had already asked if I was an exorcist, and to save a lot of laboured translation I had agreed that I was. So, when I got up, I stood behind Joe Louis's chair, laid my hands firmly on his head and said, 'Exorcism is quite simple. All you have to do is ...'

Joe Louis was off like a bullet down the stairs, clop, clop, clop, clop to the fourth floor, clop, clop, clop, clop to the third, clop, clop, clop, clop to the second, clop, clop to the first and clop, clop to the ground. Bang front door and silence. His contemporaries were rolling about with mirth.

It had turned out to be a happy evening for the Iranian exiles, and I went off to bed very much in the spirit of 'If I pass this way but once ...'.

All this was in 1989 and is an example of the new ghost interest that theology lecturers of the 1930s did not know about. Nor, indeed, were my Pastoralia lecturers to know that six months after leaving their college, and being ordained, one of their students was to meet a ghost called Tommy and many others.

After a two-year curacy in Talysarn I became vicar choral at Bangor Cathedral, and it was in this lovely old university city that my wife and I began our married life together and where our two older children, Jane and Mark, were born. It was a time when I continued to dabble a little bit here and there in the spirit world, and my wife was terrified lest I should somehow, inadvertently, bring one of the spirits home with me to Farrar Road.

In 1952 I accepted the living of what was then the plum parish of Llandegai with Tregarth and moved into our beautiful vicarage in the model village of Llandegai, where our other children, Bridget, Felicity and Sion were born, and where Zoe, our youngest, was adopted. In 1964, whilst remaining vicar of a reduced parish of Llandegai, I was appointed Director of Social Work for the diocese of Bangor. The bishop explained to me that most of the work would be with unmarried mothers and with adoption. I became the adoption officer, and my wife the very capable fostering officer, and we carried out adoptions for the then five counties in North Wales and half of Montgomeryshire in Mid Wales. Something like a thousand babies came into and went out of Llandegai Vicarage, and 500 of them were placed for adoption with new parents from the same wooden cot in the vicarage.

The bishop had said that most of the work would be with adoption, but not all. Social problems from parishes would be referred to the diocesan office and would be my responsibility. I had not been long in the post before the first call came, and it was from Jane, the wife of the vicar of Llanmynech. She phoned to say she had a problem. It was six o'clock in the evening, and her husband Robert had gone out visiting to the neighbouring village. She had no idea when he would be back. In the meantime a young couple, from the parish but not church members, had come to the vicarage looking for Robert, and were parked outside, refusing to budge until they found him.

It appeared that they both worked in Bangor; they went into the city together in the morning; and they both came home in the same car in the evening. On this particular evening they had come home as usual. He had opened the door with his own latchkey, and as they entered the hall they heard the most awful clatter coming from the direction of the kitchen. At first they thought it was a burglar, so he had picked up a cricket bat in the hall and proceeded with caution to the kitchen. Holding the bat aloft, he slowly turned the door handle and pushed. Nothing happened. The door was locked on the inside, and the pandemonium continued. When he shouted, 'Who's there?', the noise stopped. They went out through the front door and around the back. The back door was as securely locked as it had been in the morning when they had left. They looked in through the kitchen window, and the room seemed as if it had been hit by a hurricane. The contents of wall cupboards were strewn over the floor; saucepans and cooking utensils had been hurled and scattered about the room; crockery and anything else that could be broken was smashed to smithereens, and the mop and broom handles had been reduced to matchwood. And all this whilst the outside door and the inside door and both kitchen windows remained securely bolted from the inside. This they agreed could only be the work of a poltergeist, and it was, they thought, not a crime problem for the police but a spiritual problem for the parson, and they both decided they would not enter that house again until a parson came and did something about it.

'The trouble is,' said Jane, 'that when Robert does eventually come home for his supper, he will be terrified at the thought of having to go with these people to their house. Robert is scared stiff of ghosts.'

Mercifully it so happened that I had read in the local paper, only that week, a letter from an Anglesey man living not five miles from the vicarage asking those interested in forming a psychic research group to contact him. His telephone number was given. I rang him up, told him of the problem and mumbled something about its not being too convenient for me at that time. He jumped for it. 'Leave it with me. No problem.' Presumably off he went to pick up the young couple outside Llanmynech Vicarage. I saw and heard no more about it.

But the writing was on the wall. The vicar of Llandegai could dabble with ghosts and come and go into haunted house situations as he pleased. But for the Director of Social Work in the diocese, the buck stopped at his desk, and if that buck was a poltergeist or a ghost or even a demon, it was for him to deal with it.

There was, however, a choice. Swot up the problems of the occult and the paranormal from scratch or quickly make friends with those who knew about these things.

I suppose that, if my first encounter with a ghost had been horrific and frightening, I would have taken a third choice and exchanged my director's job for a quieter life in an ordinary down-to-earth Welsh country parish. But my first ghost, Tommy, and his mother were such sweet characters.

2 Tommy

Six months after leaving theological college, I was to make my first contact with a ghost, after becoming the rookie curate of Talysarn in the county of Gwynedd. Psychiatrists say that a person lives through all the experiences of life in the first five years: I have a feeling that the Revd. Roberts had a foretaste of all parochial experiences during his first two-year curacy. My ghost experience was perhaps the most pleasant of them all.

I was broken into the spirit world so very gently. Perhaps this is why I have never felt fear in any of the many haunted houses I have visited later. The first ghost I ever met was a gentle and kind ghost, and his dear old mother, before she died, was so pleased I had met him.

It was during the war, and practically every family in the village was anxious for loved-ones serving in the forces. Annie Jones was a widow in her eighties. I was particularly fond of her because she reminded me of my mother who had died. Mrs Jones had a son, Tommy, serving in the army. The old lady loved to talk about him. He had been two years in the Middle East fighting Rommel. There was no need for him to have gone because he was fifty and had already served in the Great War of 1914.

'But Tommy volunteered,' said the old lady nodding her head with pride. 'Tommy is a very loyal boy.'

He would send her a letter every week, and when I called at the cottage she would let me read his latest letters. I can remember the joy in her face when she came to tell me one day that at long last he was coming home on leave. She told the same story at the post office, and the good news spread quickly around the village. There was now a lot of to-ing and fro-ing in No.3 Coed y Brennin. Some of the neighbours

21

offered help with the food rations, and others were able to spare a few clothing coupons to buy new curtains for Tommy's bedroom.

'You will like Tommy when you meet him,' she told me a hundred times. 'Tommy is a very quiet lad – a home-lover. He likes reading – you will like him.'

Then the important letter came. Leave had been confirmed. He wasn't allowed to say when or at what port his ship would dock, but it would be soon, and his very next letter to her would be one from Britain. The old lady hobbled over to my lodgings to show me Tommy's latest letter.

Ten days later the telegram came. The War Office regretted that Thomas Hugh Jones had been killed on active service. Poor old Annie Jones looked at the telegram and let it drop onto the tablecloth. She remembered these telegrams from the Great War days. She didn't cry; she just went up to her bedroom and took to her bed. The neighbours called her doctor, but he explained that there was nothing he could do because he couldn't find anything physically wrong with her. She just lay there. A woman of sorrow, acquainted with grief. The neighbours were so kind.

Three weeks later, on a hot, sultry August Sunday afternoon, one of the neighbours came to Sunday School to tell me that Annie had taken a turn for the worse. When I entered the bedroom, she gave me a wan little smile of welcome, and I knew that she had been expecting me. I sat down on the bamboo chair by her bed and held her hand. The window blinds had been drawn against the glare of the sun, and we sat together in the quiet of the day waiting for the end. But there was a feeling in that room. It was more than waiting for the end. I knew that something was about to happen. I also knew that this was not the time to speak, that at this moment even prayers would be out of place. The window blinds rattled, and I remember wondering why, because there was not a breath of air in that tiny bedroom. Suddenly the old lady took her hand out of mine and sat up in her bed as effortlessly as a young girl would, and there was a lovely young girl's smile on her lips and her eyes were happy and beautiful. She reached out her arms and brought them together again.

'Tommy! Tommy!'

The two of them embraced for minutes on end and then, just as if remembering her manners, this new, young, glowing, happy person turned to smile at me. She clutched my arm; she clutched it by the wrist, and she held it up to where Tommy was standing. I knew she was introducing me to Tommy and if, at that moment, a hand from the unseen had touched mine, I would not have been afraid. She didn't say a word to me but her eyes told me how thrilled she was that I had been able to meet Tommy.

That afternoon I was convinced beyond all doubt that the Tommy who had been killed on active service in Africa was present with us now in this bedroom in Talysarn and that he and his mother went off together after she had introduced him to her new curate friend.

During the forty years that followed, I have sat at the bedsides of many, many dying people. No one death is quite the same as another. Some die with dignity, others without; some are just consumed by sleep, whilst others thrash and tear and fight to remain in this funny old world. But I have also seen a great number being welcomed by friends and relatives at the gates of death and joyously escorted across the Jordan.

It was many years after meeting Tommy that I was able to help another old friend who was about to die.

When I was vicar choral at Bangor Cathedral, we became friendly with our neighbours Bob and Helen Pritchard. They were older than we were but both so very kind to our two young children, and they baby-sat for us so that we could enjoy many evenings out together.

It was years later that I heard that Helen Pritchard, now in her eighties, was very ill. When I called at the old house that I knew so well, there seemed to be no one at home. I knocked and I rang the bell, but no one came, so I tried the door handle, opened the door and poked my head inside.

'It's only me. Is there anyone at home?'

I heard a faint reply: 'Oh Mr Roberts *bach*, come in, come in.'

They had brought the bed down to the front parlour, and she was propped up in a sitting position in it. Her totally bald head bore the message of unsuccessful chemotherapy, and the NHS wig was perched on its stand on the bedside table.

It had been coming on for months, she told me. She had had two operations and had been to Clatterbridge for treatment. Everyone had been very kind.

'I'm not afraid, Mr Roberts *bach*,' she said. 'But I am worried about Bob.'

'Why, Helen? Is he ill?'

'No,' she said, 'but you know how he is always on the go. He hates being in the house. I think poor Bob should have been born a gypsy. And another thing,' she said, 'Bob hates illness and refuses to talk to me about my illness, and what is going to happen to him after I am gone. He keeps saying when I talk to him, "That is silly talk. The doctor says you are getting better every day." Then off he goes on his imaginary errands to town. He is in and out, in and out, all day. I know he is worried about me.'

She asked me as a great favour if I could ring the doctor and ask if she could be admitted to hospital to die. It would be less of a shock for Bob if she could die in hospital. When I rang the doctor, he was very kind and understanding but he couldn't do it.

'I'm afraid it is too late to move her,' he said. 'The probability is that, if we moved her now, she would die in the ambulance on the way, and people would talk.'

I told her what the doctor had said, and she was quite resigned to it. But she wanted to talk about it and about what would happen to Bob. I told her about my meeting with Tommy, years before, and how he had come to take his mother away. I told her that I thought everyone should try to relax when the hour of death came, just as women were taught to relax in the labour room. If one could relax, death would be no more than the closing of the eyes in the one world and opening them in another, far more beautiful and more gentle. I told her, too, not to be afraid if the angel of death came when Bob was out on one of his shopping expeditions. I had come to understand, I told her, that men and women can lead very sad and very lonely lives in this world, but I was convinced that no one – no tramp in his hedge, no explorer in his Arctic tent, no thirsty traveller in the hottest desert – can ever die a lonely death. Those who have gone before us know the time of our departing, and they come to meet us.

'Sometimes,' I said, 'a mother or father comes to meet and to show the way to Paradise, and sometimes,' I added, 'Granny is the fetcher.'

'It is strange you should say that,' said the old lady, 'because my grandmother has been in this room with me for the past three days.'

Helen Pritchard died the next day. When I called at the house, the neighbours had taken charge. Poor old Bob was sitting in the kitchen, wiping away his tears with a dirty rag. When he saw me, he grasped my hand and started to cry.

'I wasn't in when it happened,' he said. 'She was all right in the morning, and I told her I had to go out on a little errand and that I wouldn't be long. When I came back, I knew she was dead. She looked so young. She looked just like she did the day I married her. And I shall never, never forget the lovely smile she had on her face.'

3   The Earthbound Ghost

It was in the years after the war whilst I was vicar choral at Bangor Cathedral that the big challenge came. I look back at this particular experience and regard it as my point-of-no-return in the spirit saga.

I was so inexperienced at this time that I knew nothing about spiritualism and I had never clapped eyes on a medium. The only contact that I had ever made with anything that even savoured of the unusual was the sighting of Miss Jones *Bach* in my student days and my contact with Tommy as a young curate. I had, however, made a host of good friends whilst in Bangor and established good contacts. When my real baptism in to the spirit world came, it was the power and the finances of the great British Broadcasting Corporation that was to come to my aid.

It began when members of the congregation reported to me that they suspected that some of the faithful from the Cathedral were attending meetings of the Spiritualist church over the fish shop on the High Street, on Wednesday evenings. This was the period after the war; many people had lost loved ones, and the Church was as limp and as wimpish then as it is now in its teaching about life after death. So I suppose it was quite natural that many who were bereaved were searching for solace. I know now that the founder-leader of the Spiritualist church in Bangor was Flo Litherland. She is still very much alive, at ninety-six years of age and is a wonderful old Christian who has given help and comfort to a great many people in her long life. But I didn't know this at the time, and so the young and foolish vicar delivered what he thought was a devastating sermon, aimed at those who tried to pry through the veil and refused to let their dear ones rest in peace and were a danger to the weaker brethren.

The following Monday night, when I came home from cathedral Evensong, I found three soberly dressed, middle-aged gentlemen ensconced in my study, making polite conversation with my wife, whilst awaiting my return. Their leader came straight to the point. He introduced himself and his two friends and he explained that they were elders of the Bangor Spiritualist Church, and certain things had been reported to them. I knew they had come about my stupid sermon of the previous Sunday, with its 'prying through the veil' and its 'the danger to the weaker brethren'.

'Have you ever been to a seance, brother?' asked the senior gentleman.

I had to admit that I hadn't but blustered something about having read a lot about these things, kicking myself for not having preached about something I knew more about, like Jonah in the whale's belly.

The next question was, 'Would you like to join us in worship one evening, brother? You will be better able to judge after attending one of our meetings.'

He was so right, and so polite, and I was so ashamed of myself. There was nothing I could do but thank the gentlemen for their kind invitation, and from the bottom of my heart for letting me off the hook so lightly. I asked him to give me time to think about attending a seance. The three gentlemen from the Spiritualist church took their leave very politely, their task accomplished.

The next morning I made tracks for the BBC studio in Bangor to have a chat with my very good friend Ifan O. Williams. At this very time Ifan O. was producing, for Radio Wales, weekly programmes about the unusual and the paranormal, called *Mountain Paths*. He had one about an oven in a house that had a hundred-year curse written on it for anyone who dared open it and display its contents. He had one about a perfect skeleton of a mermaid from my home town of Blaenau Ffestiniog, and I knew that he had had a very disturbing experience when he interviewed a wizard in Bala. This wizard's powers had been such that they had been able to shake even tough-guy Ifan O. himself, and he had come to tell me about this strange man's powers. It was my turn now to take my problem to Ifan O. I told him all about my foolish sermon and of the visit from the elders that followed, and that they had invited – or challenged me rather – to attend one of their seances.

Before I could say another word, Ifan snapped out, 'Don't you go anywhere near their fish-shop chapel. They'll have the whole place wired up, and they'll have tape recordings and things. They'll frighten the pants off you, that lot will. Now leave this one with me,' he said. 'I'll come back to you in a few days. I'll see to it.'

I didn't think for one moment that the three kind, polite gentlemen who had come to see me the previous night would wire the place up or frighten the pants off me, but I didn't stay to argue – I was only too pleased that morning to leave my problem on Ifan's desk.

Three days later Ifan came to see me. He had arranged it all. He told me that his first task had been to ring round and find out which was the most haunted house in North Wales, and he had found it.

When I asked him where it was, he said, 'I am not telling you, or anyone else, where it is. I know how to get there, and I have arranged for us to be there next Thursday evening.'

He had also, through the BBC, been able to engage the two top mediums in the country, both from Birmingham. These two gentlemen would travel by train and arrive at Rhyl station at 6.45 p.m. He and I and Elwyn Thomas (the School Programmes producer) would travel to Rhyl in Ifan's car, and we would also take Emrys Williams, the BBC's senior engineer, with us, and his recording equipment. Ifan had also invited two members of the Society for Psychical Research to act as referees. I was told that I could invite my three elders from the Spiritualist church, but Ifan added, 'If they're coming, they'll have to provide their own transport.' We would all converge on Rhyl station by 6.45 and pick up the two mediums, and then Ifan's car would lead the convoy to the most haunted house in North Wales.

Seven or eight people made their way past the ticket booth at Rhyl that filthy Thursday evening. They turned up their coat collars and walked off into the night. Two men followed, handed in their tickets and waited. One was a short, stocky little chap, dressed in a black overcoat and – what was even at that time, an oddity in Wales – a bowler hat. The other was a powerfully built young man, six foot and more, in a raglan mac and a brown trilby hat. Ifan nipped out to greet them and brought them back, to bundle them into the back seat of his old Austin Princess.

It was a dreadful night, rain coming down in sheets, and as if to make the effects complete, we heard loud claps of thunder in the distance. In the car we talked to the two mediums. The bowler-hatted one was a stockbroker by trade, and the younger one was a life-guard at the Birmingham municipal swimming-pool. We asked if this was their first visit to Wales, and it appeared that the older one had had a holiday in Aberdyfi many years earlier and the young one had worked one season at a holiday camp in Abergele. When we asked them if they could speak Welsh, there was quite a lot of hilarity, and they both admitted to being able to say '*Iechyd da*' and '*Croeso i Cwmru*'.

Ifan, who had been peering through the windscreen, recognized his venue, signalled to the other cars behind and stopped outside what, to us, was just a black shadow of a building. He led us all quickly up a path to the front door of what we recognized now as a rather large, double-fronted, detached house. We were obviously expected, because before we could even knock, the door was opened to us and we were greeted by two very genial ladies who were probably in their late fifties. Introductions were delayed until one of our hostesses had taken charge of our wet coats, and the other had brought in a tray full of steaming mugs of tea.

We found that the two ladies were sisters, Madge and Eileen. Madge's husband was also in the house. He was eighty-two and the sisters had persuaded him to go to bed early on this night.

Ifan introduced the mediums and told them that they were standing in the most haunted house in North Wales. The big chap said, 'You can say that again,' and just momentarily closed his eyes.

The ladies then, over tea, proceeded to tell us a little about their ghosts. Sometimes they would hear a little child crying, and Madge had actually seen a clergyman standing on the lawn holding the hand of a very pretty young lady. There was a big, portly gentleman who wore a red velvet waistcoat. (Yes, they had seen him clearly enough to be quite sure that the waistcoat material was velvet.) He had with him a

wasp-waisted young lady of the last century whom they took
to be his wife. But the one ghost that really intrigued them
was that of the old man.

It appeared that very often, when someone came into the
sitting-room, as we had that night, they could hear a voice
coming from the cellar calling, 'I'm coming, I'm coming,' and
then he would appear as a sort of misty figure from the cellar
and move into the far corner of the room. The medium
wanted to know if this figure was any specific colour, and the
ladies answered together: 'Green.' I have no idea why he was
so keen on knowing the colour, but have learnt from others
that ghosts can appear in black and white, and, very often, in
rather lovely pastel shades.

So there we were, settled in this lovely old house.
Tea-drinking and introductions over, the mediums got to
work. It was the older one that took charge.

'Ladies and gentlemen,' he said, just like a concert
compère, 'ladies and gentlemen, I want you all to feel
perfectly relaxed, because there is nothing at all to fear. We
will not have to dim the lights, and I want you all to feel free
to move around and do whatever you want, smoke, stretch
your legs or whatever. From time to time, my friend and I will
go in and out of trance. It is important, when we are in
trance, for you not to touch us. I must also warn you that
during this session one of you may feel himself falling into
trance. If this happens, don't try to fight it, just relax and let
yourself go, and my friend will look after you.'

He turned and gave a polite bow to his young colleague,
who now stood up, folded his hands as if in prayer and in a
chanting voice monotoned, 'There are some present here
tonight who have not experienced a presence from the
hereafter. For their sakes we ask for a sign.'

This, no doubt, was a reference to Ifan O., Elwyn Thomas,
Emrys and myself. I assumed the three gentlemen from the
Spiritualist church and the two representatives from the
Psychical Society would have had previous experiences. No
sooner had he spoken than two Victorian vases, perched at
either end of the mantelpiece, slowly levitated themselves,
passed each other gracefully in mid-air and exchanged places
on the shelf – left becoming right, and right becoming left.

Before they had come to rest, I was on my feet and picking

the nearest one up in my hands.

'They'll wire every damn thing up and frighten the pants off you,' Ifan had said, and, knowing Ifan O.'s reputation as a leg-puller, I wanted to test for wires. But there were no wires fixed to the vases. It was just a little warming-up trick by our ghostly friends, and the two Psychical Society gentlemen shuffled deeper into their leather chairs. It was going to be a good night.

Preliminaries over, I noticed that the stocky medium had loosened his tie; his eyes had turned upwards and were all white – deep trance, I thought. He was now clutching his head and began to cry like a child. When he came out of trance, he had to rest and complained of an awful headache. Then the young medium was off. It was just like a Russian Circus: one item was starting in the wings before the other had cleared the stage.

'Who are you, friend?' asked the older medium to the one in trance.

'I am Father Gruffydd,' came the reply, and I knew we were through to our Roman Catholic priest who had been seen in the garden. It was Father Gruffydd, not Father O'Leary or Father Patrick O'Hara – we were back in pre-Reformation Wales.

'And the lady, who is the lady?' asked our stockbroker friend. There was a lot of evasion. We drew our own conclusions eventually that Father Gruffydd had a mistress and they were either meeting in this house or living together. (This is what I find so unseemly about ghost-hunting. One finds oneself at times being so rude. I wouldn't dream of going up to a neighbour or a friend, if I saw him in a hotel lounge with an attractive lady who I knew was not his wife, and questioning him, especially before others – asking, 'Who is she, eh? Tell us who the lady is. Known her long, have you?' And yet people feel they can be as rude as they like to ghosts.)

At this point the ladies asked if we would like some coffee and mince pies, and so we readily declared an interval. The Psychical Research people were obviously well pleased with the evening and were making copious notes, and my Spiritualist elders were very satisfied with the proceedings. But we had not yet made contact with the chief character of the set-up – the old man from the cellar.

After the coffee things had been cleared, our bowler-hatted medium sat down in his chair and started to roll his eyes all over again. He was not a tall man but he was stoutish, and yet as we looked at him we could see him just as if he was shrivelling in his chair. The lights were still bright in the room, so this was not a trick. Then I looked at his face. It had suddenly become very old. There was no sign of the protruding teeth we had seen earlier. Sitting in that chair in front of us now was a wizened, toothless old man. Then he spoke.

'*Be gythral ma'r holl Saeson ma yn neud yn Fy nhy i?*' It was the squeaky voice of a very old man, and he was speaking to us in Welsh: 'What the hell are all these English people doing in my house?'

Not only was he speaking to us in Welsh but he was speaking to us in Denbighshire Welsh, and we were to learn later, from Elwyn Thomas, who is an expert on the Welsh language, that the old man in the chair was using a couple of Welsh idioms that were no longer in use even in Denbighshire.

I was also to learn later that these mediums of ours, paid for by the BBC, were considered top class because they were 'transfiguration mediums', the ones who can allow the spirit to enter and possess their bodies. Our 'I'm coming, I'm coming' old man had now taken over the body and the larynx and the eyes and the ears of our bowler-hatted medium from Birmingham.

Throughout this time the younger medium stood opposite him, his arms outstretched, as if to protect him. Now he said, 'I don't understand him. Does anyone in the room understand what he is saying?'

No one replied. I knew that our Spiritualist friends were English, and presumably so were our Psychical Research people, but Ifan O. was Welsh, and so were Elwyn Thomas and Emrys. I looked towards Ifan. He had his head down and was tapping his twentieth cigarette on the Capstan packet in his hand and examining it minutely. Elwyn Thomas had his eyes half closed, and Emrys was pottering with his tape recorder.

'He is speaking in Welsh,' I said to the man. 'I understand him.'

I looked again at Ifan O. – the chap who was producing radio programmes about the unusual; the man who, days ago, had said to me: 'They'll wire every damn thing up and frighten the pants off you.' I looked at him and wondered if Ifan had set up a candid camera situation with his friend Aelwyn as victim. Ifan O. was still busily tapping his cigarette and desperately searching his pockets for matches.

It was in the car coming home that Ifan O., Elwyn and Emrys admitted that, when the medium had mentioned the possibility of some other person in the room going into a trance, they had been terrified. This was the reason for the cigarette-tapping and the tape-recorder fiddling and the closed eyes.

'Speak to him in Welsh,' said No.2. 'Tell him that we have all come to help him.'

I didn't look at the sagging body on the chair. I was keeping my eyes on Ifan O. But I did say, '*Aelwyn ydi f'enw i. Dod yma i'ch helpu chi da ni*' – 'My name is Aelwyn. We have come here to help you.'

'*Helpu? Helpu? Be gythral wyt ti'n feddwl efo dy helpu. Tydw i ddim isio dy help di*' – 'Help? Help? What the devil do you mean with your helping? I don't want your help.'

But after this we got down to a good old chin-wag. He told us that his name was Eban Jenkins and that he was ninety years of age but still able to go about and to run his public house single-handed. He had lost his wife Gwen thirty years ago but he still missed her; there wasn't a day when he didn't think of Gwen. They had had four sons. The youngest had died aged seven, and another son had been drowned at sea when he was twenty-three. Eban Jenkins didn't want to talk too much about his eldest son. He was obviously terrified of him, but we never got to know why. When we asked if Gwen had been buried locally, he became quite irritated and said, 'Of course she is. She is buried in the churchyard behind the house here. Where else do you think?'

It was at this point that it happened. There were two BBC producers in the room, and I am sure they would have agreed that what they saw was either the best piece of acting they had ever seen in their lives or a real-life drama played by two characters from the hereafter.

Medium No.2 was nearly screaming at me, 'Tell him, tell

him, that Gwen his wife is coming for him to take him home.'
As he was saying this, I could see the second medium's eyes
turning up, and I knew that he too was going into trance. I
told the old man that Gwen was coming for him, and this
made him angry.

'Haven't I told you,' he said, 'that Gwen is dead and that
she has been buried in the churchyard over there these past
thirty years, and you go and tell me that she is ...' Then his
speech tailed off.

The fragile old man got up from his chair. He looked up to
the far corner of the room and walked towards the middle of
the far wall, his arms outstretched.

'Gwen,' he said. 'Oh! *Gwen bach ynghariad i*' – 'My love,
my love, my darling Gwen.'

They embraced. This old man and his long-dead wife
embraced in that room that night, and I could swear he wept
tears of joy when he realized that she had come to take him
home.

The Psychical Research people explained to us that what
we had seen was an earthbound spirit, Eban Jenkins, being
led to the other side by Gwen, his wife, who had come back
for him. The Spiritualist elders unashamedly wiped tears
from their eyes and pronounced that it had been a wonderful
experience.

However, Mr Becky, the Psychical Research man was not
too happy with the situation. It was a pity that I had not been
able to put many more questions to Eban. There would be
need to check, and double-check, the facts during the next
few days: the exact situation of the grave, the young son's
death and the second son's accident. We should not have let
Eban go without securing more information from him.

The ladies again brought a massive tea urn and a tin of
freshly baked mince pies. The mediums said there were ways
and means. So we all sat quietly again, and when I looked at
Ifan this time, he seemed to be fully occupied making an
inventory of the contents of his left-side trouser pocket.

This time it was the young medium who began to tug at his
tie and loosen his collar-stud. I had made up my mind that
this young man was about six feet two inches in height and
very broad. He stood up now, in the centre of the room, and
as he stood he seemed to grow until he appeared amongst us

like a giant. His lips thickened and seemed to protrude and, towering above us, he spoke in a rich, bass, Paul Robeson, 'Saunders of the River' voice.

'I am Zomba. Zomba pleased to know you all.'

It was a Psychical Research man who was first to respond: 'I am Becky. We have met before.'

We all gave our names, and Zomba acknowledged our greeting, although I cannot recall any of my three friends joining in. Mr Becky, in a quick aside, explained to us that Zomba was one of the most helpful of the spirit guides from the second stage and that he would find answers for us.

When we asked if we could recall Eban Jenkins, Zomba replied, 'No. Him now sleeping three days.'

It puzzled me that Zomba, existing in the eternal present, was able to think in terms of days. But the three days of sleeping made me think of the three days the Blessed Lord spent in the grave prior to His Resurrection.

We asked Zomba dozens of questions about the Jenkins family that night, and like a flash he would cross the great divide, look up the facts in some vast unseen library and return to us with the answers.

Eban had been ninety years old when he died, said Zomba. He had died in 'eight O'. Zomba was having great difficulty with his figures. Gwen, so Zomba had told us, had died one hundred. At first we thought he meant that she was a hundred when she died, but no, he meant that she had died a hundred years ago, and poor old Eban had been a lonely widower for over thirty years. We asked about the son who had died at sea.

'Son name Huw,' Zomba said. 'He drownded.'

'What was the name of his ship? Where did it sail from?'

Short pause. 'Ship *Anna Marie*, sail from Bristol.'

Question, answer. Question, answer. And it went on for fully half an hour. I even plucked up enough courage to ask Zomba about the little boy who cried with the pain in his head that had given our medium such a dreadful headache.

Zomba's reply was, 'He suffer what you call mene – mene – menegitis.'

Although Zomba had difficulty with the word, I was impressed with his knowledge of our medical terms. Obviously this was the Jenkins little boy who had died aged seven.

The following day Ifan and the two members of the

Psychical Research group revisited the house. They satisfied themselves that it had at one time been a public house. The ladies told them that before they renovated the house the stairs were inside. When old Eban had looked and reached with his arms to the corner of the sitting-room ceiling, he was looking towards the top of the stairs, as it was in his day, and the spot at which he had embraced Gwen was more or less exactly at the foot of the staircase. Gwen Jenkins had used her own staircase when she came back to fetch Eban.

The old man was obviously still an active publican for many years after his death. 'I'm coming, I'm coming,' was the cry of mine host tapping his barrels in the cellar and hearing a potential customer's footsteps upstairs.

Ifan told me that the churchyard was, as Eban had told us, immediately behind the house. He had traced the grave, knee-deep in nettles. It was the grave of 'Gwen Jenkins, dear wife of Eban Jenkins. Died 1850, aged 59. And also her husband Eban Jenkins. Died aged 90, August 1880.'

The Psychical Research men had explained to him that this was an obvious case of an earthbound spirit, and they had been pleased to have been present to see his release.

There were other things. There *had* been a ship called *Anna Marie* trading from Bristol, and there *was* a record that a seaman Jenkins had been swept overboard in 1846.

It was an amazing evening, but strangely enough we all turned up at work the next day, and I, at least, didn't go into great detail with the family or friends about what had happened. At that time I used to write numerous scripts for radio. On the basis that freelancers get paid for scripts but staff do not, Ifan gave me the contract to script the story for radio. A month later I had not been able to put two words together. It had been a wonderful evening, and yet I didn't know how to begin writing about it. I told Ifan, and he said not to worry, he'd get it done, but weeks later he told me that he had been up to his eyes with other work. We both thought that listening to Emrys Williams' recordings of the evening would be a help, but it appeared that, when Emrys had sat down to listen to his tapes, the day after the event, they were all blank.

It was twenty years later when John Roberts Williams, head of the BBC in Bangor, asked me again if I could sit down and write this story that I finally did so. John gave me twenty-five minutes of radio time in his Sunday evening magazine programme, and at the end of it he presented me with the tape of my story as a souvenir. I still have it.

Ifan O. and Elwyn Thomas have for some time been together with Gwen and Eban in Paradise, and in March of this year my dear old friend Emrys joined them.

Postscript
On the great night when we were all chattering about the things we had heard and seen, drinking our final cups of tea before starting off on our several journeys home, we heard an awful clatter from the upstairs region of the house.

'That must be Owen,' said Madge. 'I'll go up and see if he's all right.' A few minutes later she led the old man downstairs. 'Owen is coming to have a cup of tea with us,' she said. 'He couldn't sleep upstairs.'

She then turned to her husband and said to him, 'Owen, you remember the old man – "I'm coming." Well, these good gentlemen who have been here tonight have been able to set him free, poor thing. He has gone tonight to join his wife in Heaven, and we won't ever see him again.'

Owen thought for a bit and then he said the strangest thing.

'Well, I shall miss him,' he said. 'Every Saturday night these girls would go off to the pictures in Denbigh, and I would be here on my own. After they had gone, I would sit at the dining-room table over there, and I would tap on the table with my fingers, and then he would come and sit opposite me, and he would tap the other side. We didn't say anything, mind, but he was company.'

New and different friendships were struck in that old Denbighshire house that night. Our provincial newspaper, the *Liverpool Daily Post*, carried front page headlines about the 'Three Bangor Men In Haunted House', and somehow one drifted into a new kind of culture, a new kind of interest and a new kind of mystery that structured itself around the seance table and the meeting-places of Spiritualists.

4 Noddy

A barrister friend was telling me of his first good brief. It happened when a by-now-famous chain store was in its infancy.

The store had decided to manufacture its own sponge cake, and the packaging had been given extra care and attention. On the cardboard box container there was drawn, in colour, a picture of a most scrumptious cake, and the other side showed a succulent cross-section of it, also in colour. It showed the thin layer of chocolate, and under this the slightly thicker golden layer of marzipan, then the sponge and the cream, and under the cream, resting on the final layer of sponge, was a small red blob of jam.

It appears that some old biddy came to the new supermarket one day, bought one of their special cakes, took it home and cut it down the middle just as the cake was cut in the picture on the box. There was the chocolate and the marzipan and the sponge and the layer of cream and the sponge base. But no blob of jam. The jamless cake was reported to the Consumers' Association, and proceedings were taken against the cake-manufacturers. They had wrongly described a commodity they were selling, and giving a false description of anything that is being sold for money is an offence.

I find the only people to evade prosecution for this kind of offence are estate agents. House after house, mansion after mansion, castle after castle has been advertised for sale – all, according to them, 'with vacant possession'. Yet when the buyer finds the house already occupied by spiritual tenants, the estate agent unlike the old woman with the cake is never prosecuted, and once he gets over the shock of it, the buyer usually decides to keep very quiet about it.

When I tell people that I could be going out to exorcize ghosts from someone's house two or three times a month, they are very often mystified. How is it, they ask, that I know of so many who are troubled with ghosts, and have ghostly squatters in their homes, and yet they cannot think of a single acquaintance of their own who is troubled? The reason for this is that I am a priest and they are not.

I know of a farmhouse in which a poltergeist goes on the rampage and smashes crockery twice and sometimes three times a year. Replacements cost in the region of £100 a year. Always it is the crockery 'she' has bought, and brought into the house that is broken, never the crocks that belonged originally to the farm. The family buy the replacements and say nothing.

I know of others who come and plead, practically on bended knee, for me to rid them of their ghost. But they would say nothing to neighbours, not even to close family. When you have paid £50,000 for your semi and may be forced to sell again, it is always wise to guard your secret lest it become known to the fickle property market.

I have also thought there might be another reason for this reticence that people have about ghosts. People who have ghosts in their homes have often a peculiar sense of guilt. It is the same sense of guilt families feel when a close member is taken into a mental hospital. They will talk at length of Dad's prostate gland operation; you can often hear them boasting in the pub how their old man had his burnt off with lazer beams and not cut off with a knife; but let the old man have post-op depression or senile dementia and be marched off to the psychiatric ward in the local hospital, and the family immediately close ranks. Whatever the reason, people who live in haunted houses don't 'shout it out among the people'.

But telling a priest is different: a priest should be sympathetic. And there is something too about the confessional; the secret is somehow safe with a priest. Of course, it is also just remotely possible that a priest could help by using prayer and bell and candle and such things. So over the years I have come to know of many houses that are haunted, and very often, when the spiritual tenant has made himself a nuisance to the earthly tenant, I have been called in to arbitrate.

Some people are psychic – they are born to be mediums, to have their senses tuned to both this world and the next. They see things that others cannot see, and they hear things that others cannot hear. It is a psychic gift. Some people can divine water by holding a twig in their hand. Experience has shown me that I was never very richly endowed with these exciting gifts. This is why, whenever I go ghost-hunting, I have to ask a medium to come with me.

The first ghost job I was ever asked to perform was in a large terraced house in an Anglesey town, in 1950.

The house belonged to Peter and Bridget. They had been married six years and had one little boy, of three, and a very heavy mortgage. It was Bridget who told me of their trouble. Oliver, the little boy, was allowed to stay up until Dad came home at about 6 p.m. He would have his romps and fun and games with Dad before his bath, and be off to bed by 7 p.m. Peter and Bridget would have their evening meal, wash up together and then sit down to snooze or watch the telly.

Six weeks before they consulted me, Oliver had started to come downstairs just when Big Ben was striking nine for the news. He would just stand there with his thumb in his mouth and his eyes shut, saying nothing. At first Bridget thought he was sleep-walking and picked him up and carried him back gently to his cot. But the next night, at the stroke of nine, little Oliver again made his appearance in the living-room – not crying, just standing there.

At a quarter to nine the following night Peter crept quietly to the nursery and sat near the cot. Oliver was fast asleep. Peter heard Big Ben striking nine on the telly downstairs, and there was not a stir from the cot. He stayed another quarter of an hour and then went downstairs to Bridget. All was quiet.

It appears that a regular pattern of behaviour followed. Every night that Peter went up to the nursery, Oliver slept undisturbed all night, but on the nights Peter stayed downstairs, Oliver turned up in the living-room, thumb in his mouth and eyes closed.

It was on one of these nights that Peter took him on his knee and waited for him to wake up.

'Tell me, darling,' he said, 'why do you come out of bed like this every night?'

The little boy answered, 'Because the old man tells me to, Daddy.'

'Old man, what old man?'

'The old man who wears the long nighties and the Noddy cap,' said the little boy. 'He comes to my bed, and he wakes me up, and he says, "Go on, quick, quick now, shoo, shoo, off you go to your mummy and daddy, shoo, shoo, quick, quick" and so I come down to you.'

It was after this that Bridget had asked me if I could help.

Many people have described me as a medium and an exorcist, but I am nothing of the kind. If there were such a thing as a psychic vibration meter, I would score zero. I have entered dozens of houses with mediums to see the poor things holding their heads in agony as strong psychic vibrations throb through their bodies. I have seen my medium friends pinned against walls by spiritual forces. But I have never in my life experienced a single vibe or been thrown about. A good medium can make a ghost show himself, and when this has happened and others have gasped at the sight with awe, I have remained blind. A ghost has to be pretty cheeky and extrovert before I become aware of his presence.

I say this to explain why, on all my ghost inquiry expeditions, I have to be accompanied by a medium. It was my medium friend who suggested we go to the nursery in Peter and Bridget's house. We all tiptoed upstairs. I knew from the pained look on the medium's face that the vibrations were strong and were hurting him.

Oliver was fast asleep in his little bed, in the far corner of the room. The medium walked up to the bed, clutching and shaking his head as he got nearer. He then walked to each corner of the room and stood for a time in the corner opposite the bed. He whispered to us: 'If we can move the little lad's bed to this corner, he'll be all right.' Peter and I dutifully picked up the bed, with Oliver in it, and placed them both down where the medium indicated. Oliver kept on sucking his thumb, and the rest of us went downstairs.

'I don't think you will be troubled again,' said the medium. 'The little boy's bed was just in the ghost's path where it was. It will be all right now.'

This will probably go down as the quickest ghost job I have seen carried out! The whole thing took about twenty minutes flat, and although I checked several times with the parents, Oliver's nocturnal perambulations came to an end on that particular night.

I have come to the conclusion by now that ghosts can bore me. I never did read ghost stories or subscribe to psychic magazines. The greatest penalty of being a ghost-hunter is that people come up to one on the high street to relate some corny incident they remember which happened to some distant member of their family.

But the one thing I still enjoy about ghost-hunting is the careful checking, and double-checking, of everything one has seen and heard on a good night, when contact has been made. I must confess that for this kind of detective work I make full use of my clerical collar.

After our pleasantly short visit to Peter and Bridget's house, I decided to call on my friend the vicar of the parish. I told him about the problem we had come across in the house and asked him if he knew who the previous tenants were. He didn't, but he knew the charming old lady of eighty-six who lived next door and who had a wonderful memory. Armed with a tape recorder and my clerical collar, I decided to call on the old lady. The clerical collar gained instant admission to the house.

Yes – the old lady remembered a good number of people at No.42. She herself had been born in No.41 and had lived there ever since.

'People don't seem to stay in 42 for long,' she said. 'I don't know why that is, but things are different these days. Young people seem to be always on the move, changing jobs and bettering themselves.'

She went through a large catalogue of the previous tenants: the Browns and the Erskines and the Donovans and that lovely couple whose names she couldn't remember. After about an hour we were down to the tenants of the 1900s. (This was 1950, remember, and the old lady would have been thirty-six at the turn of the century.)

'It must have been around 1900 when old Captain Lucas moved in,' she said. 'He was a tiny little man and he had two lovely daughters, Lucille and Victoria.' I pricked up my ears at this – 'the tiny little man' part, not the daughters.

Old Captain Lucas, it appeared, had made his fortune as a

'captain-owner' trading in the White Man's Grave – Africa. He had come to the town to retire and had brought his two daughters with him. There was no mention of a Mrs Lucas; people assumed he was a widower. Lucille and Victoria had confided to their next-door neighbour many times that they were bored with their drab life in Wales and missed the colourful life of Liverpool.

To make matters worse, the old man kept a jealous eye on his two lovely daughters. If one of them looked twice at a young man, their father would bristle. Miss Victoria had actually made friends with a young man, who, one day, decided to call on her at No.42. After he had left, her father had gone into a fit of temper.

'He is only a cheap fortune-hunter,' he ranted at her. 'If you dare even to set eyes on him again, I will disinherit you. Do you understand? Not a penny will you get if you even look at that whipper-snapper again.' Then poor Miss Lucille and Miss Victoria had been sent to their rooms.

'Did the Lucas family stay long?' I asked.

'Oh, about four or five years, I would say,' said my old lady. There was no stopping her now. The Lucas era was all flooding back. 'Old Captain Lucas was very fond of his drop of whisky. Very fond of his "Be Joyful", Miss Lucille used to say. And the young ladies got into the habit of carrying bottles of whisky in to him. People say that shortly before his death he used to drink two bottles a day. At that time he didn't even dress himself. And the young ladies were afraid of anyone calling to see him.'

'Because he was always drunk?' I ventured.

'Oh no,' said the old lady. 'That was the funny thing about Captain Lucas. Drink didn't seem to affect him. I never once saw Captain Lucas drunk.'

'Why were the girls ashamed then?' I persisted.

'Well, because he used to be around the house all day in his long nightshirt and his funny cap.'

I knew we had arrived. 'Funny cap?' I said.

'Yes,' said my old friend. 'He would even go out into the garden in his long nighties and his "sleeping hat".'

'And what kind of hat is a "sleeping hat"?' I asked.

'Well, it is a long hat shaped like a cornet and with a tassle on top.'

'A hat like a Noddy hat,' I said to myself. So it's old, bad-tempered Captain Lucas who was shooing the little boy down to his parents every night!

It appears that after their father's private funeral the Misses Lucas had come home, packed their bags and gone off in a hansom cab to catch the 2.30 train back to Liverpool. No one in the town ever saw them or heard from them again.

I passed no.42 the other day. There was again a huge notice in the garden: 'House for Sale with Vacant Possession'.

People should not be allowed to contravene the Trade Description Act.

5   A Rustle of Ghosts

There is one large house in Bangor that must be the estate agents' dream. No sooner is one family settled in and the 'Vacant Possession' notice carted away than it is back on the market again. It is a lovely period house, solidly built; it surveys well, and it obviously sells well. I have noticed recently that the new buyers are always from away, so I can't be the only one in Bangor who knows it is haunted. In one sense it is not true to say that it *is* haunted. It might be fairer to say that it has a ghostly lodger who keeps himself, or herself, very much to himself, or herself.

I have told my family about this house but have warned them to keep silence, and so very often one or other of the children will come home from town and tell us that the big house has had new tenants again. We then glance across, as we come home on winter evenings, to see it glowing with bright lights and warmth as the new family overruns all the rooms with their tellys and their homework and their toys and their hobby-making rooms. Then, in perhaps three or four or sometimes five months, we begin to notice that the light in the room immediately over the front door is not switched on as often as it used to be; another short period and the room is in constant darkness.

We at home know the reason for this, as I am very friendly with an ex-owner of the house, and I also know a lady of eighty-six who was born in that house and lived there until she married.

'Oh! It's haunted all right,' she told me. 'Daddy would never allow us to enter that bedroom over the front door. Believe it or not,' she said, 'I have never seen the inside of it. Not even when we cleared the old house after my parents died. It was always locked, and Daddy had the key, and we never talked about it. The rest of the house was warm and snug, but that room, and even the landing that led to it, was cold and horrible. We all had the feeling that whatever possessed it was nasty and evil. Sometimes, possibly about twice a year, we would hear a wailing noise coming from the locked room, and then pandemonium would break out. The noise was the kind you would expect if someone was breaking the furniture into matchwood, though I never heard Father say anything was ever broken. But it was a nasty, spiteful ghost we had in there. Mind you,' she would end, 'I have never said a word about this to anyone except you, of course.'

My friend who lived there for a couple of years, ten years ago, says the same thing, and he also adds, 'Mind you, I haven't said a word to anyone about it.'

So there seems to be a code of honour about these things, apart from risking the depreciation of the value of the property to the owners. Possibly all vendors of haunted houses have a sense of guilt that they have not declared the possession to the purchaser, and when the purchasers in turn become vendors, they feel a moral obligation to maintain the secrecy.

I have been very lucky and have never come across a nasty ghost. I have even felt quite sorry for some ghosts, and I don't think it is right for people to exorcize some ghosts from homes they have occupied for a very long time. I do know, on the other hand, that there are these nasty, vicious, evil ghosts. There are a whole army of poltergeists, some childishly playful, others attracted to homes and places where young children congregate. I have never met a poltergeist or an unpleasant ghost.

W.R., a clergyman colleague of mine, described to me in great detail how he battled throughout the night with a demon spirit.

He was a country vicar, as I was. He was married and had two lovely children. The bishop offered him the delightful parish of the Old Priory. The priory itself was a semi-ruin, but the prior's house stood intact and was to be home to the new vicar and his family.

W.R. was a great DIY enthusiast, and he knew that,

notwithstanding the zeal of the Diocesan Parsonage Board, every aged building in their care needed a great deal of resuscitation before it could house a new family. He therefore decided to pack his tools, roll up a sleeping-bag and precede the family to the Old Priory. His plan was to renew, repair and refurbish the rooms that would come into immediate use when they moved in.

The priory boasted one huge front bedroom overlooking the bay. 'This,' said W.R., 'shall be the master bedroom.'

That night, after oiling countless locks, fixing dozens of curtain rails and repairing the lavatory stopcock, the new master trundled his way up the stairs to sleep his first sleep in the priory by the sea.

'I was tired,' said W.R., 'and I think I got off to sleep very soon. It was a warm, sultry August night, and I slept on top of my sleeping-bag.' It must have been about three o'clock in the morning when he woke up. 'I was stiff with cold, and I was scared. I remember lying there trying to remember why I was scared and what it was that scared me. Then I heard it. I can't remember whether it was the noise of its breathing or a peculiar pulsating wheeze, but I turned my frozen body to look towards the large old fireplace. It was then that I saw it. The fireplace was black, and he, sitting against it, was blacker, so that I could see it – the outline of it against the fireplace – and its white, watery, malevolent eyes. He was like a huge, horrible, slimy octopus, and he was going to kill me with his eyes,' said W.R.

'I tried to turn my face away but I couldn't, and I knew from his eyes that the beast knew that I was his prey and that I could not escape. Then I thought of Maria and little Jimmy and Meg, asleep in the other vicarage, and the beast shouldn't have let me think of Maria and Jimmy and Meg, because it was then that I decided to fight. I tried to stand up, but my body was too cold and too stiff. Then I tried to bring my right hand to my forehead to make the sign of the cross. I got it as far as my throat, and I crossed my chest with the sign of Jesus. I tried to speak, but only a croaking noise came from my lips. I knew it to be "In the name of the Father and of the Son and of the Holy Spirit." The beast also recognized the words, because his white eyes burned the more into mine.

'All that night,' said W.R., 'I babbled my prayers:

'Our Father which art in Heaven ...

'O Holy Jesus, most merciful redeemer ...

'God be at my end and at my departing ...

'I was forgetting my prayers, then the one from my childhood came to me,

Gentle Jesus meek and mild
Look upon a little child.

'And the psalms – I could still remember the psalms:
"I will look up into the hills from whence cometh my help."

'The psalms were easier to remember. "... though I walk through the valley of the shadow of death ..."

'I was determined to keep it up. My teeth were chattering, my body was frozen, but I kept it up. Every second of every minute I kept on praying to God.

'And throughout this time the beast was glowering at me. He was breathing and vibrating, and those vibrations were entering my body, suffocating me, and then I could hear myself saying over and over again,

"Jesus keep me till the morning.

"Jesus keep me till the morning.

"Jesus keep me till the morning.

'And then suddenly it was morning, and I was alive, and my body was becoming warm again, and the devil beast had gone, and I knew that he would never, never return to the priory again.'

Jacob wrestled with an angel, but W.R. wrestled with the devil himself and won, and the large priory bedroom overlooking the bay would after all become their master bedroom, and there would be no need for little Jimmy and Maria ever to know that on his first night in their new home their Daddy had fought a battle to the death with the spirit of evil.

After hearing this story from W.R., I checked with two other incumbents who had lived in the priory. I asked them if the place was haunted. Had they seen a ghost there?

'No,' they said, 'you couldn't say that the priory was haunted.' No, they hadn't actually seen anything, but what had prompted me to ask about a ghost, they wanted to know.

'Did you sleep in the big front bedroom overlooking the bay?' I then asked them.

They both answered, 'No. We kept that as a sort of spare room – a sort of lumber room.'

Now I have seen the big front priory bedroom overlooking the bay, and I think that a man would have to be either very crazy or very scared before he would designate a beautiful room like that a lumber room.

It makes one wonder what kind of human being would, after death, turn into a poltergeist. I have thought and thought about this one. My experience, talking to ghosts and listening to what they say, leads me to believe that the fact of dying makes no difference to our personality or beliefs. When we die, we close our eyes in this world and open them in another – a world which, if those who have died and been clinically resuscitated after peeping at it are to be believed, is very beautiful. But our personality, our ego, our self, in that brief act of shutting our eyes in one existence and opening them in another does not change. A nasty, bigoted, dirty-minded loud-mouth closing his eyes in this world will, in the next existence, still remain a nasty, bigoted, dirty-minded loud-mouth. The only difference is that he will be clad not in a physical, carnal body but in a spiritual body and will have the makings of a nasty, bigoted, dirty-minded, loud-mouthed ghost.

It is good practice when ghost-hunting, and when conversing with ghosts, not to mention historical dates. Ghosts are very vague about Anno Domini. Also they are not too keen on describing actual places – there seems to be a ghostly code of practice that dates and places are not things to be discussed, in the same way that money is not regarded as a subject for conversation amongst the better bred. So in a ghost conversation, in order to orientate oneself, questions have to be asked about the prime minister of the time, or the name of the vicar of the parish. More than once, after entering into this period of enquiry, one comes across a spirit who spits at the name of Gladstone and offers three great cheers for good old Dizzy. I would imagine that a good number of Cavaliers in the afterlife still nurture great hatred for the Roundheads. Earth characteristics and earth bigotry seem to remain for a long time after death.

It is in this way that I try to explain to myself the spiritual chemicals that must go to the making of poltergeists.

We know of football vandals who after matches go on rampages, breaking and tearing apart and terrorizing people. Young people with a cruel, warped nature. Recently I heard about two young lads up before the magistrates in Llandudno for acts of vandalism inside the church. They both admitted to having urinated on the altar. They had wanted to hurt and degrade all the people who worshipped and made their communion together in that church. I couldn't help but think that, if these two had been struck dead on that night, we could have been left with two strong, lusty, nasty-minded poltergeists ready to tear up and desecrate some home or school or church. I am glad I have never had to deal with these vandal ghosts and evil spirits.

When I received a visit from a warden of a college hostel some years ago, I did think I might have to deal with one. He told me that at the beginning of the October term a girl student had fled in terror from her bedroom. She had been awakened by the sounds of frantic scratching on the window. She looked towards the window and there, outside, she saw the horrible face of an old lady who looked like a witch, clutching the sill, grimacing to her to open the window and let her in. The poor girl fled from the room and never, ever, she said, would she enter that room again, not even to pack her bags in daylight.

It was a mixed hostel, so I suggested to the warden that he might offer the room to one of the boys.

'I have,' he said. 'I offered it to the captain of the rugby team, and the first night he ran down the corridor starkers, shouting his head off.'

Three others had tried and failed, and now the whole six-bedded wing of the hostel had had to be closed. The warden wondered if there was anything I could do, because the loss of six rents was one the hostel could ill afford.

I promised I would go and speak to the students after supper on a Sunday night. The hall was packed. The home students were all present and correct, plus a great gathering from neighbouring hostels. I gave a little talk about the habits of ghosts, told them of the ghosts I had come to know, told them there was little to fear, that I had never heard of anyone physically injured by a ghost and that they had to remember that the ghost had prior claim to the building. He or she had probably lived there before the students were born.

'My advice to you, if you see this ghost or any other ghost,' I said, 'is to keep calm and speak to them. "Who are you? Can I help you? How can I help?"'

After my little talk the warden asked for questions. A young freshman, a theological student, jumped to his feet. He was white with anger and very nearly frothing at the mouth. How could I, an ordained priest, dare to dabble in the spirit world? He went on to quote verse after verse from the Old Testament, condemning and bringing curses on the head of all those who 'called up the dead'. Poor little fellow, he was trembling with anger!

I had to remind him that I was only doing what the Blessed Lord had done before me. When Jesus had taken Peter, James and John to the Mount of Transfiguration, he had met Moses and Elijah – not the physical Moses and not the physical Elijah, because they had been dead for several hundreds of years. Jesus met the spirit, or the ghost, of Moses and the spirit, or the ghost, of Elijah, and Peter said: 'It is good to be here. Let us make three tents. One for Thee and one for Moses and one for Elijah.'

I also told the student that if I, a priest, could show someone just one ghost/spirit, I would have gone a long way to showing there is, indeed, life after death. The students gave me a loud ovation for all this. I think they felt it was rude of the new student to have made such a vicious attack on a guest speaker.

When I heard the poor little fellow's outburst, I knew his secret. There is so much to learn, and so much I don't understand, about this ghost business that it is comforting when experts lay down for one at least a few proven, basic facts that one can use as a plumbline or a geometrical theorem. One such theorem is, 'No ghost can manifest itself without the assistance of two mediums, one on each side of the divide.'

This old lady college ghost had possibly had an obliging medium on the other side for some time, but there hadn't been a helpful medium amongst the college hostel inhabitants. At least not until our angry new student had arrived a few months before.

I knew about this phenomenon because a friend of mine,

who later became my curate, had told me about it. Apparently he was one of a family in South Wales called 'the Oak Tree Family'. No one knew why, unless it was to do with a peculiar gift they had of being able to smell death. He would know just by passing a terrace of houses if someone was to die during the next three days. I have known times when we both knew of a parishioner who was near to death, but often he would say no to that area and point instead to another neighbourhood where to the best of our knowledge there would not even be a hospital out-patient. Often within the three days we would hear of a motor-bike fatality or some other unexpected death.

He would conduct a mid-week celebration of Holy Communion with just a handful of parishioners present and then come and boast to me how full his church had been that morning. His parents had been there, Edward, the old church warden was there, Mrs Williams, Sling, was there, and the old bishop who had ordained him, and a host of others. He was a medium all right but somehow had managed to cope easily with this extraordinary gift.

He told me that the last night before he left home to go to university his widowed mother had told him to come in early because she wanted to talk to him. He had gone to say goodbye to a friend, fully expecting on his return a long lecture from his mother about drink and always to treat girls with respect and not to gamble like some students did. When he at last came home, and he and his mother sat down together to a cup of tea, his mother simply said,

'Roger, I want you to listen carefully to what I have to say. If some of the students decide to play around with a ouija board or they start telling fortunes with cards or mind-reading or anything like that, I want you to promise me that you will leave the room at once and have nothing to do with such things.'

She knew that her son had strong mediumistic powers, and she was warning him of the dangers.

The other student's mother had probably not told him of his strange gift. It had been with him all the time – something to be kept down and repressed; something to feel guilty about; something to hide. Then along comes this clergyman, this so-called priest of God, saying he had spoken to ghosts, encouraging the students to speak to ghosts and being quite blasé about the whole thing, and something had snapped.

'How dare you, a priest of God, dabble with the spirits of the dead?'

Our angry student had arrived at the college as a freshman in the October term of that year. The old lady ghost had been seen also that term. I hadn't the courage to tell the student that the ghost was a camp-follower of his and that probably there would be many more over the years. I did, however, tell the warden that, if he was worried about losing the rents for the east wing, he should consider finding good hotel accommodation or good, homely lodgings for his angry student.

It all seemed so simple, and people who had sought help and advice were so very relieved and so very grateful. It was worthwhile work and I began to feel that there was nothing to this ghost business. Pride comes before a fall.

6 *The Learner*

My introduction to the medium world had been something of
a baptism by fire. My experience with Eban Jenkins had been
like that of a novice hooking a two-pound trout with his very
first cast. I had, somehow, gone in too deeply and too soon. I
couldn't even read the road signs.

All this happened in the early sixties and at a time when
more and more people were coming to me with ghost
troubles. It was quite obvious that many of them were very
frightened and very unhappy people. I kept thinking of the
two Birmingham mediums of years ago. They had been so
efficient and so professional in the way they had tackled the
case of poor old earthbound Eban Jenkins. I realized that this
kind of social/spiritual social work was not for the dabbler or
the do-gooder, nor was it for those of little knowledge like
me. I decided that if help was to be given it would have to be
the help of an expert. I would have to know more about these
spiritual invaders from the world beyond – I would have to
become a learner.

On that particular evening, whilst the medium, sitting away
from the rest of us, was coming out of trance and stretching
out his arms and quivering, a little kitten sitting on the arm of
the settee got the idea that he was trying to stroke her, and
she nuzzled closer and touched him. The poor chap nearly hit
the ceiling. All the professionals were apologetic that they had
not anticipated the cat's action, and they all agreed that it
was a jolly good job that he was coming out of, and not going
into, deep trance when it happened – 'Or else ...' they said.
'Or else what?' I didn't discover. There was so much
happening that night I didn't dare ask. Strangely enough it
was ten to fifteen years before I got the answer to my

question. It was then I heard of the first Spiritualist martyr who was burned to death by being touched.

Helen Duncan, a Scotswoman, was a most gifted medium practising her art in the 1940s. She was arrested in 1944 and charged (under the Witchcraft and Vagrancy Acts) with pretending to have mediumistic powers. Helen Duncan's defence was that she wasn't pretending anything of the sort but that she actually did have special powers, and she asked permission to give a practical demonstration to the court. Permission was not granted, and she was sentenced to nine months imprisonment and also had to undertake not to practise, or pretend to practise, mediumism again.

In 1956, at a private seance in Nottingham, she was persuaded by friends to take part in a demonstration. The police had been keeping a watchful eye on her since her first conviction, but it does seem as if some informer had given them information about the Nottingham seance. The police raided the house at a time Helen Duncan was in a deep trance. In spite of warnings from those present, two police officers laid hands on her to arrest her. She collapsed in their arms and was rushed by ambulance to hospital. She died in hospital thirty-six days later. The post-mortem showed that she had died of severe burns to her body and especially in the region of her solar plexus – the area mediums regard as the body's main seat of ectoplasm.

Helen Duncan's death caused a great stir throughout the country. Air Marshal Lord Dowding and Hannan Swaffer, both adherents of the Spiritualist Church, and Morris Barbanell, founder and editor of *Psychic News*, activated the press, and many questions were asked in parliament. The young Spiritualist Church laid claim to its first martyr.

I had been puzzled earlier why there had been, seemingly, so few ghosts in Blaenau Ffestiniog, when I was a child. I knew now that the ghosts were there – legions of them, as there are today, only at that time there were not the mediums to act as escape vehicles for them.

It is almost inconceivable that as recently as 1950 – 1 December 1950, to be exact – members of parliament debated for a whole day the repeal of the Witchcraft Act 1735 and the Vagrancy Act 1824, and the introduction of a new act, The Fraudulent Mediums Act, which the

Spiritualists welcomed, to take their place. During the debate Mr Monslow, MP for Barrow in Furness, was able to show that mediumship was first practised in Britain in 1853. It appeared, too, that those who did practise mediumship were often arrested and charged under the Witchcraft Act or the Vagrancy Act, as people obtaining money by pretending to have occult gifts. The case of *Duncan v Hill* was quoted, and members agreed that it had been unfair for Helen Duncan not to have been given a chance to demonstrate her 'gift'.

From 1853 until the repeal of these acts, mediums kept a low profile and practised in a hole-and-corner manner in small sanctuaries in private houses, and in unmarked 'churches' or 'centres'. The ghosts were there all the time, but they began to make their appearances only when mediums multiplied in the more tolerant age that followed the repeal of the Acts that had previously been used for their persecution. 1950 saw the emancipation of the Spiritualist movement.

More than anything else, it was the Spiritualists' teaching about earthbound spirits that terrified me. My whole nature rebelled against this grotesque idea. And yet I had seen 90-year-old Eban Jenkins, who had been buried under a tombstone that had his name on it, still carrying on as a publican in North Wales, ninety years later. Spiritualists were now telling me that some people – not many, but some – died a clinical death, cast off their earthly bodies, put on their look-alike spiritual body, began to move forward and then unexpectedly failed to find the ford in the River Jordan, the pearly gates or the tunnel with the beautiful music that so many resuscitated dead had described. They became lost, helpless and earthbound.

The idea of losing the way on my death journey terrifies me. I have never been quite sure which is my right and which is my left. When I sat my driving test, many years ago, I had to ask the examiner if he would kindly point with his pencil the way he wanted me to go rather than say left or right to me. Whenever anyone gives me road instructions, I invariably miss a turning, and maps are no use to me.

I have never been afraid of real death, and my contact with the unseen has strengthened my belief that death holds no danger for any of us. Some of my friends, however, are terrified of death. I have seen so many people, in hospital and in their homes, fighting, thrashing and screaming useless protestations against the angel of death. Does one tell people that there is a greater fear than the fear of death itself – the fear of not being able to die, of being earthbound, of being part of the Flying Dutchman Syndrome?

I then had a hard think about all the funeral services I had taken, the number of times I had recited the committal: 'We commend the soul of this our brother to God the Father Almighty, and commit his body to the ground, earth to earth, ashes to ashes, dust to dust, in sure and certain hope of the resurrection to eternal life, through our Lord Jesus Christ.'

Some clergyman must have said these words over the coffin of Eban Jenkins. It was probably true that Eban had had eternal life, but what kind of eternity was it if it meant going on and on and on tapping beer barrels in the cellar until my friends and I, quite by chance, were able to find the soul of his wife to show him the crossing place?

During the past twenty years of my ministry the great theme has been the idea of reunion.

'Let us join with the Methodists,' the Evangelical bishops say.

'Let us not ordain women to the ministry lest it become a stumbling-block to our reunion with the Roman Catholic Church,' the High Church bishops would say.

But I never heard even a rural dean saying, 'Let us join with the Spiritualists', and the Spiritualists seem to have so much knowledge about this great facet of truth in the Christian world – eternal life.

Mediumism was first practised in 1853 but it was not until the aftermath of the Great War, 1914 – 18, that the country realized that a new Church, one which gave regular demonstrations of its belief, had been born. Thousands of people throughout Europe had lost loved ones in the war, and the Anglican Church, in spite of the Oxford Movement, had never been able to find anything to replace the burning candle, and prayer for the dead, that Luther had taken away. People in their thousands turned to the new Spiritualist Church, not to join but to attend occasionally and perhaps be lucky enough to receive a message from a dear one.

The 1920 Lambeth Conference, no doubt concerned about

this new teaching and its following, set up a commission of two archbishops and thirty bishops to report on the Christian faith in relation to Spiritualism. It was told: 'It is possible that we are on the threshold of a new science which ... will confirm us in the assurance of a world behind ... the world we see, and that a limit could never be set, to the means which God could use, to bring man to the realization of a spiritual life.'

But nothing was done.

Later, in 1938, Archbishop Lang appointed another committee to inquire into Spiritualism. For some unknown reason, the Archbishop locked away the committee's report in a safe at Lambeth Palace. Somehow Morris Barbanell, editor of *Psychic News* had a copy spirited to him – what we today would call a leaked report. Archbishop Lang's committee had reported to him that their investigations had shown that, 'Communications of the spirits, with people on earth, was a fact.'

By 1950 the Spiritualist Church had grown considerably. Mr Paget, MP for Northampton, asked the question in the House, 'What is the Spiritualist movement?'

Mr Monslow, MP for Barrow in Furness, replied: '... there are 1,000 churches affiliated into two main organizations, the Spiritualist National Union and the Greater World church. The active membership is 50,000, with thousands of other adherents. At the National Conference in London in 1948 forty-one countries were represented.'

By 1950 the Church had amongst its adherents members of parliament and well-known personages such as Air Marshal Dowding, Sir Arthur Conan Doyle, Hannan Swaffer, Alfred Russel Wallace and Marshall Hall.

Another member of parliament, anxious to give respectability to a movement that had been persecuted for some time, quoted from the Mass Observation Inquiry conducted in 1947 (the equivalent, no doubt, of our present-day Gallup Poll). Parliament was told that, of the people questioned,

35 percent believed in Spiritualism
36 percent believed in ghosts
51 percent believed in second sight or clairvoyance
64 percent believed in intuition
86 percent believed in telepathy.

I remember that about that time, when all these questions were being asked about the Spiritualist Church, my own bishop in the diocese of Bangor, Bishop J.C.Jones, who knew that I was flirting with the Spiritualists and loved, in the privacy of his study, to hear my tales of ghosts, asked for my opinion of Spiritualism. I could only say to him what members of the archbishop's commission had said to the archbishop: 'Communications of the spirits, with people on earth, is a fact.'

But I knew that I would never be able to find a home in the Spiritualist Church. Their whole concept was too narrow; there was the over-concentration and the specialization on just the one of the thousands of facets of the teaching of the Blessed Lord. It would be just like going to church and listening to the same sermon every Sunday. I was anxious now to break away from the religious mediumship and meet some of the lay, freelance mediums I had heard about.

When my next call for help came, I had the pleasure of working with a Spiritualist medium and a researcher with exceptional psychic gifts under the same haunted roof.

7   The Renaissance

It was in the early 1970s that I attended my first Spiritualist service. A Spiritualist service is structured very much like an Anglican service or a Methodist service. It has the same main sections – readings, prayers, sermon and messages, only they call their sermon, 'the Philosophy'.

At the service I attended, Bob Price was the medium, and he was reputed to be good. We'd had the prayers and the readings, and we were now awaiting the Philosophy from Bob. He started off with 'Dear brethren in the Lord' when something happened to his voice – it became a funny, high-pitched squeak, but he still continued to speak. Bob's deep baritone voice had been replaced by an old, cracked, high-pitched cackle.

'Greetings to you, friends. I am Ting Lem, and I have many good things to tell you.'

One of the more knowledgeable in the congregation said to the rest of us, in a sort of aside, 'He is a Tibetan monk, of hundreds of years ago. We are very lucky to have him present.' With that, he turned around and cleared his throat and addressed himself to the empty chair in front of him: 'Greetings to you, Ting Lem. I am Burroughs. We have met before.'

Then came the reply: 'Ting Lem pleased to see Bullos.'

Then everyone in turn introduced himself to the monk and was acknowledged. When my turn came, I said, 'And I am Aelwyn Roberts. Pleased to meet you.'

'Ting Lem pleased to see Alw Lobots,' came the reply.

After the introduction Ting Lem took over completely, using poor old Bob Price as his mouthpiece. He told us he had joined our circle that night because he knew we were worthy and capable of understanding great knowledge. The cracked old voice then went on for about twenty minutes telling us about the joy of true tranquillity, how it is possible to listen to total silence and how a man can train himself to listen to the pure music of nature. Quite honestly, I was very disappointed with the whole thing. I felt that Bob Price, left to himself, would have done so much better, and I said so.

'If that Philosophy came from a Tibetan monk who has had many centuries of learning and meditation to aid him, I don't think much of it.'

Bob Price was now out of his trance and was anxious to know what had happened and what he had said. I quoted the television magician Paul Daniels' catch-phrase to him, 'Not a lot.' My friends thought I was too hard on poor old Ting Lem. It was Bill Peters, a member of the Society for Psychical Research who proffered an explanation. A spirit from the other side, he told us, could only be as intellectual, fluent and effective as the medium he was using as his vessel of communication.

'Tonight,' said Bill, 'Ting Lem was using Bob Price as his communication instrument.' He then turned to Bob and, in front of us all, asked him, 'How did you get on in school, Bob? How many "O" levels did you get?'

Bob gave a prompt reply: 'Two – scripture and woodwork.'

Then Bill Peters turned to me and said, 'That's your answer – Bob's two "O" levels.' Peters went on to say, 'If we had had Bertrand Russell or Oliver Lodge or Hannan Swaffer in Bob's chair tonight, then by golly we would have had a philosophy of a lifetime.'

That may be true, but I must say that up to the present I have never received a single message, from any of the departed, that has been of any practical help to me in this life.

Seances at this time were only for the brave and the daring and for those who were so bowed down with grief that they were willing to venture all. Hypnotism was also something that savoured of the dark and the unfriendly. The eyes of all would be instinctively averted from the hypnotist lest evil should prevail. I should, I suppose, say that the eyes of all were averted except the eyes of those living in my little parish of Llandegai.

During the mid-fifties and throughout the sixties, our village was served by two greatly loved general practitioners. At this time, most babies were born in their own homes and not in hospital. When the expectant mother felt that her time had come, she would summon the district nurse, who would then arrive at the home with her little black bag, and in the fullness of time she would summon the doctor. As our two village doctors took alternate night-confinement duties, the expectant mother would not know, until the hard labour stage began, which doctor would actually deliver her baby.

The younger of the two doctors was a great admirer of Dr Dick Read of 'Revelation of Childbirth' fame. Dick Read taught that perfect relaxation in childbirth abolished pain. The African women he had observed would just walk into the jungle, crouch down and drop their babies, effortlessly and painlessly. When the Dick Read fan doctor of Llandegai entered the confinement bedroom, the command would be, 'Out of bed and crouch down on the bedroom floor.'

'If, however, the older partner was called out, his first action would be to disengage his gold watch and chain from his waistcoat pocket and swing the watch gently in front of the patient's eyes, saying the usual formula, 'You are becoming very tired. Your eyelids are becoming heavier and heavier. You want to close your eyes.' And the baby would be born without stress to himself or pain to his mother – under hypnosis.

This, of course, was hypnosis practised by a greatly loved medical practitioner. The general tendency however, was to shun such practices by lay persons, except perhaps for the demonstrations that were making their appearances at variety concert halls up and down the country. A great change of attitude came in the 1950s and 1960s. This was the renaissance period for all who worked in the field of the paranormal. It was a time of great experimentation and new discoveries were made almost daily. A vast army of mediums, sensitives, hypnotists and others interested in the occult, who had previously been working in secret, were now able to show themselves. It all happened when the hated Witchcraft and Vagrancy Acts were repealed in 1950 and replaced by the far more sensible Fraudulent Mediums Act. The flood-gates were open and almost immediately the study of the paranormal, in all its forms, became a respectable science; people living in ordinary houses began to declare their ghosts; men and women endowed with sensitive or mediumistic gifts were able to offer them help without the fear of prosecution as witches, wizards, or vagrants. The disciples of Dr Mesmer became known as hypnotists and a new word 'hypnotherapist' was added to the vocabulary of the man in the street.

Sigmund Freud had discovered the unconscious mind, and had left much for others to think about, to talk about and indeed to quarrel about. Freud had demonstrated that a great deal of mental illness was the result of the locking away of early fears and phobias in this newly discovered unconscious mind. Over the years such fears would slowly fester and eventually break out into recognizable mental illnesses, depression, hysteria, paranoia and the like. Freud also laid down a form of treatment. The original hurt, fear, phobia, or wound that was the cause of the illness would first have to be identified and exposed. This could be done by his system of psycho-analysis and it involved patient and therapist undergoing long painful sessions of questions and answers. These sessions could only be terminated when the patient himself was persuaded to look at the wound in his own mind and acknowledge it as the cause of his lack of well-being. Freud had many followers throughout Europe and his ideas of the unconscious mind and his new system of psycho-analysis was received by doctors with a greater ease than many of the innovative medical ideas of the past. The snag, however, was the time-consuming treatment. Psycho-analysis required of the therapist hours and hours of manipulative questioning. Very often drugs would be used to facilitate the seeking of the hidden wound. But Freud also showed that during sleep the guardians of the secrets of the unconscious mind were less vigilant than they appeared to be in the waking period. Secrets and hidden thoughts heavily disguised, were able to enter the patient's dream world.

This new knowledge was something that the hypnotherapist was able to turn to his own advantage as a health practitioner. The hypnotist already knew the art of inducing sleep and had also mastered the art of enabling patients to regress through the past to commands given by the therapist.

It was soon discovered that as the regressed patient came near to his hurt area, he would become agitated and disturbed. One therapist told me the story of a male patient of forty who had regressed under his instruction until he had come to the time of his actual birth. He had then started to tremble and to cry like a baby before suddenly twining his arms as if to protect his head. He had then shouted out 'Mind my bloody head – mind my bloody head.'

Later medical checks disclosed that he had been born a 9 lb 6 oz baby to a young mother with particularly small pelvic bones. 'She' had caused him great hurt, but 'She' at this time was his great love and the centre of his whole universe and could not be blamed. So this great hurt that he had suffered had to be put away, hidden out of sight, in the place that Freud called the unconscious mind. The doctor ventured the opinion that if his patient had been born by caesarean section he might not have needed to see a psychiatrist forty years later.

It was at this time in the 1960s and about ten years after Roger Bannister had broken through the four-minute mile barrier, that I first heard of another great barrier breakthrough – this time in hypnotic regression. For all I know this could have been something practised by the ancient Egyptians, or the Greeks, or the Incas hundreds of years ago, but I first heard of it happening in Cardiff and the Roger Bannister of the Hypnotherapy Regression barrier was a man called Arnall Bloxham. This man had set up his clinic as a hypnotherapist healer in Cardiff at the end of the Second World War. His fame as a clinician spread very quickly. He was invited to give public lectures, made many appearances on radio and television and was known throughout Wales as a successful healer. The BBC even produced a television documentary about his work and his experiments. Bloxham would induce his patients into a relaxed state and then encourage them to regress back through time recalling incidents from their past lives – even down to the period of childhood. The therapy questions and answers were all carefully recorded on tape.

One day a patient regressed past the childhood stage and beyond the memories of birth to the very end of memory. After a very short interval the patient began very clearly and very deliberately to describe another life in another country and at another period of time. The therapist asked questions that required detailed knowledge of the place and period and received the answers from his patient, and all were recorded on tape. Arnall Bloxham, since his childhood days, had believed in the teaching of reincarnation (that people after death are born again to live other lives on this same earth). The evidence of his tapes, where all of a sudden one patient after another were describing to him their other lives, appeared to him to be proof manifest of what he had always believed. The tapes were used in lectures to demonstrate the fact of reincarnation. Bloxham as a sort of corollary to his theory of reincarnation also believed that skills learnt in one life could sometimes filter through to another, this would explain the many child prodigies in the world of music and the arts, and the many geniuses of science.

I wrote to Arnall Bloxham at this stage, but I don't think I got a reply. What I tried to tell him was that I had seen and heard demonstrations similar to those he had on tape. The presentation was similar, but the conclusions that we came to were very different. I told him about the bowler-hatted medium from Birmingham who presented himself to us as an old Denbighshire publican and had even spoken to us in an outdated Denbighshire dialect. As Eban Jenkins, the publican, he had told us the place of his wife's burial and the next day we had found it. He told us of his son's drowning, and the name of the ship, and we received corroboration of this from the shipping office in Bristol. In the interview we heard little details of Eban Jenkins' life that only he would have known, and yet the stockbroker medium from Birmingham would not have dreamt of claiming that he had lived on this earth before as a Welsh publican. Bob Price would have been flabbergasted if any one suggested to him that in some other life, many centuries ago, he was Ting Lem, a Tibetan monk. These two men would have said that all they did was to move up a little inside their bodies, and make room for another spirit body to enter their physical frames and use them for a little while. The spirits would then move out and they would become themselves once again.

I know, too, how my medium friend Winnie Marshall sets up her canvas from time to time and takes out her brushes and paints and working like an expert she will execute a superb landscape. Winnie would never never wish to make the claim that in a previous life she was Michelangelo or Constable. She tells me that she is just the person who holds the brush; it is one of her artist guides who moves it across the canvas. She admits that without the guide she would not be able even to draw a picture of an egg.

Bloxham's reincarnation teaching worried me greatly at this time. I began to think that Bloxham's Theory of Reincarnation would perhaps rock the Church as much as Darwin's *Origin of Species* had a century earlier and I wondered who would champion the Church against what I thought of as the Bloxham Heresy. At this time I knew of no other priest that dabbled with ghosts, mediums and seances and I needed such a person to talk to and to exchange ideas.

Coming home from a harvest thanksgiving service in Anglesey, I turned on the car radio. It was a programme about hypnotism. The hypnotist had commanded a young lady volunteer to regress to the age of six. She was reciting for the listeners, in a small, childish voice, the recitation that had won a prize for her at the Urdd Youth Eisteddfod thirty years earlier. She also recalled a great deal about other Eisteddfodau of the time and about Eisteddfodic bards, adjudicators and compères long dead. I listened at the close of the programme for the name of the hypnotist. It was Elwyn Roberts. I made up my mind that I would have to meet this Elwyn Roberts.

8   *Council House Ghost*

I had been visiting friends and was making tracks for home when a boy of about ten came up to me. He was pale and very agitated.

'My mother is not very well. Will you come to our house?'

When I arrived at the house, it dawned on me who the little boy was. He was one of Eifion and Eileen's six children, and I wondered immediately what could have happened to Eileen. She was sitting in the kitchen, just staring straight ahead, with a sort of incredulous look on her face, and her whole body was trembling.

'What's the matter, Eileen?' I asked. 'What is it?' She just continued to stare at the blank wall. 'Are you in pain?' I tried again, and this time I got a slow response.

'I – have – seen – a – ghost. He – was – standing – just – there – and – I – saw – him.'

One of the neighbours came in and made tea all round; that seemed to revive Eileen and distracted her from staring at the wall. When we had drunk our tea, I asked her to tell me what had really happened.

'It was a few minutes ago,' she said, 'and I was expecting the children to arrive from school. I was sitting on this chair and had just finished mending Eifion's shirt and was putting my mending things away when I looked up and there he was.'

'There was what?'

'There was this man standing there and looking at me.'

'Did you know him?' I asked.

'No, he was a strange man – never seen him in my life. I don't think he was a man. He was a ghost.'

'Describe him then,' I said to her.

'He was a stocky man of about fifty. He had a large black moustache, and he was dressed in old-fashioned clothes, sort of Teddy Boy clothes, and he had something white on his head.'

'Did he speak to you?'

'No, he just stood there in the hall, just stood there and stared at me – well, not *at* me really, just *through* me.'

'And then?'

'And then he just disappeared, just melted away,' said Eileen. 'It's as simple as that. He just melted away.'

Eileen was getting over her shock now. The other children were coming home from school, and she made a very brave effort to pull herself together.

'I must make tea for this lot,' she said.

I'm quite sure that Eileen will not disagree with me if I say that Russell Grant, the television astrologer, would have described her as one of those born under the star that shines on the more romantic. Eifion, her husband was of a very different nature – the slow, quiet, practical type, and I wondered how he would react to this situation. I decided to call again in the evening, after they had all had their tea and Eifion was home. When I did call, the children had had their tea and had gone out to play again.

'Has Eileen told you of her experience this afternoon?'

'Yes,' said Eifion. 'She's told me.'

'Well, what do you think about it?' I asked.

Eifion's reply was, 'I was only waiting for this to happen – for Eileen or one of the children to see him. I knew that as soon as they did, the balloon would go up, and now it has.'

Eifion then went on to tell me that he had already seen this ghost three times in the last six months.

'The first time,' he said, 'Eileen and the children had gone down the road to see Gran, and I had volunteered to wash up the tea things.'

He told us that he was nearly finishing the drying when someone passed the kitchen window.

'I thought it funny because it's only the children and the neighbours who come to the back door, and although I had only a glimpse of this man, I knew he was a stranger. So I dried my hands and moved towards the door to open it and see who it was. But I needn't have bothered,' said Eifion. 'Our ghostly friend was already in and standing right there in the kitchen door opening. He was just staring at me.'

'What did you do then?' I asked.

'There wasn't much I could do,' said Eifion, 'because he was blocking the only exit from the kitchen. I couldn't make a bolt for it. And anyway, I don't think I was afraid. He was sort of looking beyond me, and I looked at him.'

'For how long?'

'Difficult to tell really. Long enough for me to have a jolly good look at him. He was the same bloke that Eileen saw, all right. He was a short, stocky, thickset man. Huge shoulders and a sort of bull neck. He had a huge black moustache, and he also had a heavy gold chain running across his tummy. And,' added Eifion, 'he had something white, like a turban, on his head.'

Another night, when Eifion was on his own, he had been reading and had decided to make himself a cup of coffee. When he got to the kitchen, the ghost man was there, just looking out of the window.

'He didn't even turn round when I entered the kitchen,' said Eifion. 'I don't think he can see or hear us. He thinks he's in an empty house.'

I don't think Eifion would have minded sharing his kitchen with the moustached ghost, but enough was enough for Eileen. She wasn't going to have a ghost for a lodger. We tried many things – such as hanging a crucifix in the kitchen. I even celebrated communion in the kitchen, but it made no difference. The spiritual tenant was appearing more and more often, and he was making himself known to the children.

I phoned the Elwyn Roberts whom I had heard on the radio regressing the young woman back to the age of six. He was kind and he was helpful.

'You tell me that there is a family being troubled by a ghost, and you want me to help,' he said. 'Now I don't want you to say anything more about it. Don't tell me a word about the kind of ghost it is. It will put me off completely if you tell me.' Then he added, 'If it is convenient for you, I shall pick you up at your home at seven o'clock on Thursday evening, and if you don't mind, I would like to bring a friend of mine along with me – she is Mrs Winnie Marshall and is a good medium.'

*

That was how I first came to meet two very good friends of mine, Elwyn and Winnie, and it was a friendship that was to bridge the years. It is quite amazing the friendship that one can form, in just a few hours, working with others on a ghost problem – somehow all inhibitions go, and so do the formalities.

After our council house session I lost track of Winnie Marshall for many years. By the time we renewed our acquaintanceship, she had become a much-sought-after demonstrator at meetings up and down the country and also in many countries in Europe, and she had also to be treated now with greater reverence because by this second meeting she had been made a minister of the Spiritualist Church.

Elwyn and I were to go on working together over the years. It was not just our common interest in the paranormal. We had long talks about theology, Anglican Aelwyn and Methodist Elwyn. We talked books and poetry, about Elwyn's experiences in his research work and about hypnosis and its uses in therapy.

I entered the world of spirits almost by accident, but I think Elwyn was born into it. I remember his telling me how he used to have 'out of body experiences' at the age of five, and at the age of eight he would hear voices, not in his head but whispering his name in his ear, and he pretended the voices were fairies. And his books, from an early age, were about poetry and electricity and the unexplained mysteries of the Bible. I have often been amazed at the depth of his understanding, and his search for knowledge, and more than anything at the way in which he accepts, with humility, the strange gifts that have somehow been thrust upon him. There has always been that understanding that, however busy either one of us is, when a real, urgent call comes, we always make ourselves free to respond.

One Thursday evening the Parry family evacuated their council house home. The key was under the mat, and Elwyn, Winnie and I found our way in and got ready for whatever was to come. Elwyn and Winnie agreed that there was a strong presence; something would happen. The three of us chatted for quite a while and got to know one another.

In the middle of the conversation, Winnie started to sway slightly, and she was very quietly humming a little tune. Elwyn and I kept quiet and watched. Winnie clutched her head and rocked it in a violent nodding movement, then in a deep, booming voice she gave a sort of desperate cry, 'My het, my het, I feel as if I haff had a stroc.' Then she slumped down in her chair like someone who was going into deep sleep. But she roused herself, and within minutes she was with us again and perfectly normal.

We recapped on what she had said. The deep voice suggested a man. 'My head, my head' suggested that there was pain, only she had said, 'My het, my het' and the 'I feel as if I haff had a stroc' suggested someone with a foreign accent – a German, maybe. The ghost was perhaps the ghost of a German who had been injured or was in pain.

After a fairly short recap of the situation, Elwyn decided that he would have a go, he just allowed himself to relax. I don't quite know how to classify him. The trance that he floats into always seems so shallow. Ghosts don't seem to speak through him: they just come up to him and obviously talk to him, because he will say, 'He or she is saying this or that.' He will then say to me, 'Go on, Aelwyn, find out what you can. Ask your questions.' Some sensitives who enter a trance state have to ask those in the room what has happened and what has been said, but Elwyn seems to be perfectly conscious throughout the session. I often wonder why he needs me, why he doesn't ask his own questions.

Elwyn said to us in a very quiet voice, 'I see him in my mind. He is a short, stocky man in his fifties. He is well dressed in an Edwardian suit, with well-polished shoes, and he's got a thick gold watch-chain across his waistcoat. He is in great pain, and he has what I think is a white towel wrapped around his head, and I think there is blood on it – yes, it is blood, and there is blood on his suit as well. Talk to him, Aelwyn.'

So off I started on my little bit: 'Tell us who you are? Give us your name.'

Nothing.

'We have come to help you. How can we help?'

'Hold it,' said Elwyn. 'He is saying something to me. He is terribly earnest about whatever he is saying, but it is in some foreign language and I can't even think what language it is.'

I remember thinking at the time that, although Elwyn was a scientist and not a linguist, had the spirit spoken in French, Spanish or Italian, he would probably have at least spotted the language, if not the meaning, but this was a more uncommon foreign language.

'It's English now,' said Elwyn. 'He is asking me to forgive him. No, not me, he is asking everyone to forgive him. He has been punished, and he is still in great pain, but he deserved the punishment, he deserved the pain, because he had betrayed his people. He dare not move from the place because the hounds of hell are awaiting him.

'Speak to him, Aelwyn,' said Elwyn. 'He is a very sad man.'

That night, in that council house, I preached a sermon on salvation and on God's mercy and forgiveness to a penitent sinner. I told him not to be afraid to move on, because it was his Heavenly Father who was beckoning him.

Elwyn said, 'He is smiling. There is a little smile on the sad face, and he is walking away from us. He is leaving us.'

There was nothing more to do for the three of us knew we had accomplished our task. I went two doors down the road to ask Eileen and Eifion to join us. When Eifion came into the room, he beamed and said, 'You've done it. The old chap has gone. I can feel it.'

Winnie Marshall laid her hands on Eifion's head. 'Do you know, lad,' she said, 'that you are one of us? You have good, strong mediumistic powers.' Then she gave him advice: 'No house that you live in will ever be free of ghosts. Wherever you live, you will see ghosts where others see nothing. You attract ghosts. Learn to live with your gift, my lad, and for the sake of others always keep your own counsel.'

And so, after cups of tea and long chats, the ghost-hunters made their way home.

For Elwyn and Winnie it had been a good night. By their God-given gifts they had helped a spirit, most probably an earthbound spirit, and they had been able to release him from his pain and from loneliness. For them it had been a satisfactory evening. But I still had my problem. This terrace of council houses had only been built in the 1930s, so why should one of the houses be haunted by a stocky man in Edwardian clothes, and particularly by a foreign gentleman in Edwardian clothes – and not just a French or Italian or

Spanish foreigner but the kind of foreigner that even Elwyn could not recognize.

I picked up an Ordnance Survey map, pre-1920, and was convinced that I would find that a little farm or a smallholding had nestled once where the estate houses stood now – but no, the site was just a field. I spent hours asking people and looking through old census papers, but I could find no explanation as to why the ghost of a foreign gentleman from the Edwardian period had come to find himself injured and earthbound in a 1930 council house in our little village.

By this time the media had moved in. There were ITV cameras inside and outside the little house. But the reporter fraternity are very practical, very earthy: I don't think a single one of them showed any interest or asked any questions about the ghost – a ghost is a ghost, for all that. What they wanted to know were the practical things. Was the district council prepared to re-house this family? If they did rehouse the family, would they then re-let the house to another family? Did the council intend calling in an exorcist? Provincial papers of Wales had a heyday, and I was told that one particular reporter made a nice little bonus selling the story of the council house ghost to some American magazine. And all this time I struggled to find some kind of explanation.

I met a friend of mine whose father, now a good age, had lived in this part of the village all his life.

'Ask your father,' I said to him, 'if he can remember if there was a house or a shed or a workshop or anything on that patch of land before they built those council houses on it.'

The following evening he rang me up.

'I've asked the old man,' he said, 'and he told me that there was never a house there but that at the end of the Great War, 1914–18, when he was a teenager, some Russian and Polish foresters came to live in temporary huts there and cut down the trees on the little hill behind them. And just where Eileen's house is now, he says, they had their sawmill.'

I have never understood why Russians and Poles came to our little village in the Ogwen Valley to cut down and mill our trees, but they did. Many of them married local girls, and there are Russian surnames on our tombstones. So our foreign gentleman had been a Russian or a Pole, and it was perhaps not to be wondered at that Elwyn, the scientist, had been confounded.

My friend's father had gone on to say that, when these Russians had cut down the trees at the top of the hill, they would then sit on the trunks and ride them as sledges at breakneck speed down to the sawmill at the bottom. Many of them had serious accidents doing this, but it didn't seem to deter them – they still went on doing it.

My friend kept his father's memory gem to the last. His father remembered very clearly how one Saturday morning there was a rumour in the village that one of the Russians was missing. He remembered how thrilled he and the other boys were to see the one police Ford saloon car, with five helmeted policemen squashed inside it, arriving at the Russian camp site. The policemen spoke to the other men in the camp, opened some shed doors and looked inside; then they all went back in their saloon car again.

Now I was satisfied. I had had my answer. I concluded that the Russians and the Poles lived in a close-knit community in the village, keeping themselves to themselves. In some way our ghost friend had betrayed or harmed his compatriots, and it must have been something really mean, despicable beyond words. There had been a kangaroo court, and the betrayer had been found guilty and brutally lynched, and his body hidden in the saw mill. There had been a sparse search by wartime, part-time constables, and the affair was closed.

The story of the council house ghost with its neat ending, which the newspapers had missed, made a great story for John Robert Williams' Sunday evening magazine programme on radio.

A week after the broadcast, a local solicitor came up to me on the high street.

'My wife tells me,' he said, 'that you broadcast a story last Sunday evening about the ghost of some Russian man who was murdered in the village. I wish I could have heard it,' he said.

He went on to tell me that when he was doing his articles with a firm of solicitors, they had on their books, as a client, a Russian gentleman who was a patient in a mental hospital in Devon. (I didn't try to solve the mystery of how it came about that a firm of reputable solicitors in North Wales had such a client on their books.) It appears that this client would write a letter to his solicitors twice every year. The contents of the letters were just pure, unintelligible gibberish, but my solicitor friend remembered that the final paragraph of every single letter was the same:

'Please pray for the soul of my father who was killed by his own countrymen in a small village near Caernarfon. Pray that he be saved from the torments of hell fire.'

9 The Smelly Ghost

Our calls usually come from individuals troubled in their own homes. Most will have waited until the bitter end before seeking help. I suppose people feel foolish picking up a phone and speaking to a perfect stranger and asking if it is possible to come and see him and to talk about a ghost. And I suppose, too, that, having called at the vicarage, it must be difficult to start talking about 'our ghosts'. People do all this only because they are very desperate.

The person who came to see me about the Smelly Ghost wasn't even living in the same house as the ghost, nor did he intend to, but he was a very worried man. He was the secretary of a local housing association which had bought a rambling old house on the outskirts of the town. The intention was to turn it into five luxury flats for letting. The house had been empty for some time and had items of the original furniture stored in it. Male members of the housing association committee had volunteered to clear the house. It was at this early stage that they began to think that they had a problem on their hands. The house was unnaturally cold. One of the men said that, if bricks and mortar were capable of emotions, this house, on the night they moved out the furniture, was actually hostile. It seemed to be ganging up against them. One member of the committee kept saying that there was someone behind the hedge watching them, but it was when two of them started rolling up the carpet in the cold room that trouble had really started. When the carpet had been rolled half way across the room, the two men had very nearly been suffocated by a most horrible stench and had staggered out to cough and gasp in the yard outside. An hour later, when others entered the room, the smell had gone. Boards were lifted, just in case a body had been buried under the floorboards, but there was nothing. That night the trailer was overloaded, and some odds and ends were left in the house, because no one wanted to have to make a return journey to the big house. No one mentioned ghosts.

They carried on with their normal duties the next day. They needed time to think. They had a problem on their hands. The house had been bought and paid for, contractors' tenders had been accepted, and the building work was to commence the following week. Committee members decided that the less said, the better.

The following Monday at 8 a.m. the contractors men came on the job, and by 11 a.m. they had downed tools, walked out and refused to walk in again. They said that the bloody place was haunted, and it was so cold inside that they could not grip their tools.

Members of the housing association decided to go and have a chat with the last tenant to live in the Big House. If it was haunted, they thought, surely Edgar would know about it. He saw them coming up the front drive, and before they could say anything to him, he said, 'So the workmen have seen the little lad, have they?'

He confirmed their worst fears. They did have a ghost on their hands.

Edgar then told of his own experiences whilst living there. There were always doors banging when they shouldn't have been banging; there were certain no-go areas that became cold and hostile at certain times; and there was the little boy. When Edgar, his wife and their young children had first moved in, they all heard the sound of a child crying. Many a night he or his wife would wake up to the crying of a child and rush off to the children's bedrooms, only to find them all fast asleep.

Then one day Edgar had seen him. When he was working in the garden, he looked up and saw a little boy of about ten standing on the front door step. He described him as having blond, blond hair, nearly white, and eyes that were unnaturally, penetrating blue – blue eyes like nothing he had ever seen before. He called out to the little boy that all the children were out, for the boy looked so normal that Edgar took him to be a friend of his own children. (It was only when he told the story later that he realized that the boy's clothes were a little old-fashioned.) The boy, still looking over his shoulder at Edgar, walked into the house. Edgar called him back, but the little boy defied him and ran upstairs, with Edgar in hot pursuit.

Up the first flight they went, and up the second. When the boy dived under a bed, Edgar gave a loud 'Got you' and made to grab his legs. Then suddenly he was engulfed by some kind of vapour and a most horrible smell that nauseated him. He rushed downstairs and had to stay in the garden for some time to steady himself. When he went back to the top bedroom, all was perfectly normal and tidy, and there was no trace of any little boy or a smell.

Since that date both Edgar and his wife had seen this little boy in the house many times, they had often heard him crying and there were times when they had heard a ball bounced against a wall and gone into the backyard to find no one there. The children had said that they had seen two blue, blue eyes staring at them through a slit in the garden fence.

'So,' said Edgar. 'I'm sorry lads, but you most certainly have a ghost on your hands. The little boy is quite harmless,' he said, 'but I'm afraid that there are a good number of other ghosts in that house as well as him.'

The contractor persuaded his workmen to return to work, and the members of the housing association committee kept their counsel. But in one week the men were out again. This time it was the smells. At first they thought it was the drains, but then it got much worse. One morning, when they were all having a break in the small downstairs room, there had been a little, ploppy noise and a little cloud of mist, and after that a horrible smell like 'bloody poison gas'. They had their own ideas about the smell. There could be no explanation, they said, except that a body had been buried underneath the floorboards.

Members of the housing association committee immediately thought of the little crying boy: what if someone had murdered him and buried his body under the floorboards? Concealing a ghost was one thing, concealing a dead body another. The committee decided to call in the police. Boards were lifted up in several rooms, and a thorough three-day search was made.

Bones, covered in lime, were found under the floorboards

in one room. Forensic, however, decided that they were the bones of a cat and not of a human, and someone came up with the information that in olden days people did bury their pets inside the house.

It was after all this kerfuffle that the chairman of the housing association came to see me, to ask for help.

'If you could only get rid of the smell,' he said. 'My colleagues and I are now convinced that, even if the men do go back to work and we do get the flats finished in time, this smell is not going to go away and we will never be able to let them to tenants.'

So that very night I rang Elwyn, and a date was fixed.

When we arrived at the chairman's house, on the appointed night, we found the whole committee there, ready and eager to accompany us. Elwyn chose the chairman and two others and told the rest that we would report back to them two hours later. As usual, Elwyn had no idea what we were looking for. Man ghost, woman ghost, old ghost, young ghost? He just wanted to find out for himself.

It was a November evening, cold and dreary. The house was bleak and miserable, and the only light we had came from a couple of candles and a small calor-gas lamp. But we didn't have to wait long before the performance began. Doors started to bang and rattle, and the candles flickered, and then Elwyn told us that there were dozens of characters wafting in and out of the room.

'I see a very attractive young lady,' he said, 'and I have a name – it is either Anwen or Rhian. She is in her early twenties and rather sad-looking. Outside in the garden I see two army officers dressed in navy blue or black uniforms, and they have crossed swords on their epaulettes. The young officer is kneeling before the older man, and he seems to be pleading with him. The name that comes to me for the younger man is Harold or Harry Grange. He has three stripes on his sleeve, and I think he is a captain. The older man has a much higher rank, possibly a general, and I have the name Stephenson, John Stephenson.'

Elwyn thought that perhaps the young officer was pleading with the older officer for the hand of the young lady, Anwen, in marriage. He does later see Anwen and the officer together, and they look sad. He also sees her walking under an avenue of yew trees to a church by the lake. (The local men recognize the description of the church but not the yew trees.) There is also another character: he has modern clothes, navy blue jersey and trousers, and a sailor's cap.

Elwyn says, 'He is a sailor and yet not a sailor, and his name is Richard Jones.' Richard Jones seems to waft in and out of all the scenes.

Elwyn then announced that there was a party going on. The people at the party seemed very articulate, and the ladies' dresses were ornate and beautiful. The high officer, John Stephenson, seemed to be the host, and the young officer, Harry Grange, and Anwen were trying to sneak out to the garden to be alone together, but others seemed to follow them. About half the male guests seemed to be army officers, and they all paid homage to a very elderly general. Elwyn got the name as General Harold, and he asked several times for a surname only to have Harold repeated but this time with the rank General Harold. Elwyn also said that there was much talk of someone called Antler who was an army officer. He had the impression that this was a farewell party, because some of the officers, including the young Captain Harry Grange, were going on overseas duty, and Elwyn could see Indian buildings and Indian scenes in the background.

When Elwyn and I went downstairs for a short break, I saw him flung against a wall. He was pinned there for three or four minutes, looking just as youngsters do when they go on the Wall of Death gravity rides at showgrounds, only Elwyn was towering over me and looked about seven feet tall.

Our friends of the housing association had made copious notes of all that had been seen and heard during the session, and we all decided, as it was so cold, to return to the chairman's house for a cuppa and a recap on what we had seen so far.

The locals had apparently expected us to come up with crowds of ghosts, and they weren't surprised to hear about soldiers. Modern Richard Jones, 'a sailor and not a sailor', was a new one to them. When I recalled how Elwyn had appeared to grow to seven feet tall, they remembered Edgar's telling them how, one evening, he had dozed off in front of the telly and woken to see an enormous man towering over him.

When we mentioned the church that had the yew trees, one

of the committee was able to tell us that the church used to have a yew tree avenue; it had been chopped down but the stumps were still there.

It was arranged that one of the committee should be responsible for sending the names of the officers we had met that evening to the curator of the Royal Welch Fusiliers Museum in Caernarfon. Captain Harry or Harold Grange, any service in India in or before 1860, and John Stephenson or Stevenson, an officer of high rank, possibly a general. General Harold –? 'Antler'?

The replies were as follows. Regarding the first query, the curator pointed out that our information about him was not strictly accurate – he obviously expected the same accuracy from a ghost as he would from a regimental sergeant major!!

My researches have failed to reveal a Captain Harry Grange. However, as you say, the information in your possession may not be accurate in all respects. In view of this there is one officer who could qualify as the subject of your investigation.
Assistant-Surgeon Henry Grange, 47th Regiment of Foot
Born at Portarlington, Queen's County (now County Kildare), Ireland on 1st May 1833. He entered the Army as an assistant-surgeon and served on the Staff, and subsequently in the 47th Regiment (later the Loyal North Lancashire Regiment) in the Crimean War from 13th November 1854 to the cessation of hostilities in 1856. He was present at the siege and fall of Sebastopol, and at the attack on the Redan on 8th September 1855. Grange was detached from his regiment for special services in India during the Sepoy Mutiny of 1857–1858, and was in medical charge of a Squadron of the 2nd Dragoon Guards at the action at Azimghur on 7th April 1858 on which occasion his horse was shot. The 47th Regiment later proceeded to Canada and was stationed in that country before the end of 1861: it is presumed that Grange would by then have rejoined the regiment. Assistant-Surgeon Grange was dismissed the service by order of a General Court Martial on 17th April 1862. His name was struck from the Army List from that date.

Despite the fact that there are obvious discrepancies concerning the rank and Christian name, the age appears to be approximately correct (Grange would have been 27 years old in 1860). Furthermore he was a member of the medical department and would therefore have worn a blue uniform, but not insignia consisting of crossed swords. You will be aware, I am sure, of the danger of making established facts fit a particular series of circumstances. However, I cannot help but feel that the above information could be relevant in this instance.

If I can be of further assistance then please do not hesitate in contacting me, but in any event I should very much like to hear of any further development in this most interesting matter.

(Signed by the Assistant Curator of the Royal Welch Regimental Museum.)

It appears, too, that we had over-promoted the older officer.

Lieutenant-Colonel John Stephenson, 17th Lancers
His date of birth is unknown but it is assumed that he was born in the late 1790s. He joined the 17th Lancers as a private soldier and accompanied the regiment to India, where he served from February 1814 to 1823, including the campaign of 1817–1818 against the Pindarees. Appointed to the regimental pay section on 30th April, 1847. Commissioned cornet, 16th February 1844; lieutenant, 25th September 1845; appointed paymaster, 30th April, 1847; appointed paymaster to the Cavalry Depot at Canterbury, 24th November, 1857; honorary major, 1st April, 1860; honorary lieutenant-colonel, 8th September 1870; to half-pay, 28th September, 1870.
Major Stephenson served with his regiment in the Crimea (1854–56) and was present at the battles of Alma, Balaclava (where the 17th Lancers took part in the famous Charge of the Light Brigade) and Inkerman, on which occasion he acted as Adjutant to his regiment.

We managed the proper rank for the general, but Elwyn had been incorrect in questioning whether the Harold was Christian name or surname.

Major-General John Casimer Harold
Commissioned ensign, 14th Foot, 25th September 1806; lieutenant, 28th May 1807; captain, 74th Foot, 16th February 1815. Transferred to the 2nd Royal Veteran Battalion; major, 11th Foot, 10th January 1837; lieutenant-colonel, 11th November 1851, retired on full pay; colonel, 14th April 1857; major-general, 1st July 1858.

This officer served in the Peninsular war and was present at the Battle of Corunna (16th January 1809) for which he received the medal and clasp.

The Museum officials set a test question. They said to our researcher, 'If you have a further session, please ask this question of your clever medium, "For whom is Antler a nickname?"'

When we did meet the second time, Elwyn gave the prompt and apparently correct answer. Antler was a nickname for John Stephenson, and of course that was why there was so much talk of a person called Antler at the party – but no one saw him because we did not associate the name with that of Colonel Stephenson, who hosted the party.

We are all very grateful to the staff of the Royal Welch Regimental Museum at Caernarfon for their help, and for their continued interest, because up to this moment none of us has any idea why so many important army officers met in this little North Wales town in 1857 or thereabouts to attend a regimental going-away party. We are working on it.

In the meantime, however, I had to break the news to Elwyn that, although, probably, the first night had been a good night, we hadn't come within a hundred miles of tracing the nasty smell and the little boy and that this was really our first commission.

Elwyn is a very kind, patient person but when he heard about the little boy I'm sure he must have felt like strangling me.

'Oh! Aelwyn, Aelwyn! Whatever possessed you to get a party of old cronies like us together and expect a little boy of ten to come and join us? I ask you, what little boy of ten would like to drop his play and come and talk to a decrepit old parson and his mates?'

I said I was sorry, and we got down to it to make fresh plans.

Elwyn asked if the others thought that Edgar, the previous tenant, and perhaps Edgar's wife could be persuaded to join us at the next session. A runner left the house for the Red Lion and within seven minutes came back with Edgar in tow. 'Yes,' Edgar would come. 'No,' he didn't think his wife would come. So a date was fixed and we all went home.

At Session 2 we had the same company plus Edgar. Elwyn knew this time that he was trawling for a little blond, blue-eyed boy. He persuaded Edgar that it would be easier for the little boy to join us if he would allow himself to be hypnotized or put into a shallow sleep. Edgar agreed to this with a promptness that surprised all of us.

The first person who appeared was our Richard Jones – the sailor who was not a sailor, just walking vacantly on and off. Then a woman came and gave her name as Elsie Jones. She had with her a little boy of about four with very light yellow hair and very blue eyes. She was dressed in the style of the 1930s and had blonde, bobbed hair. The woman went out and came back again several times. Then she walked up to Elwyn, pointed to the little boy and said, 'He was drowned when he was eight years of age, in the lake where the boats are.'

Not one of us can remember why, but we were all agreed that the little boy had been drowned in 1938. Then Elwyn came through with his corrections. I am never sure how he manages these, unless it is through one of his two guides. The corrections were: for Elsie Jones read Elsie Craddock, and the drowning did not occur in the town.

Elsie Craddock was a Welsh woman who had married an Englishman. They lived in Manchester – even the area, Eccles, was given. Their blue-eyed little boy had been a cub scout. (Elwyn could see him in cub scout uniform.) He had fallen off the jetty, between the jetty and a boat. Richard Jones – the sailor who was not a sailor – was his uncle and was somehow connected with the accident. The little boy's name was Robin Craddock, and although he lived in Eccles, in Manchester, he obviously spent a lot of time in this little Welsh town with his friends Alun and Huw. Robin could even speak a little Welsh.

When he came to us, he was obviously bouncing a ball; we all heard the bouncing but saw nothing – strange. He told Elwyn that he had bought the ball and a top when he went on an outing to Llandudno.

I have never known Elwyn lose his cool, even when he is in trance, but at this moment he jumped to his feet and shouted at us, 'This little boy has been drowned. He is dead. I can see a black hearse and this little boy is in a tiny little coffin in the hearse.'

Elwyn began to cry, and we looked at Edgar, who was still asleep but sobbing quietly, with tears running down his cheeks, and then Elwyn's crying was taken up by the crying of a child at the far end of the room, and the crying got further and further away from us, and then it stopped. Elwyn told us that Elsie Craddock had caught up with her little boy. 'He won't come back again,' he said.

The housing committee members had come to us, in the first instance, so that we could salvage their investment for them, but by now they had all become enthusiastic psychic researchers. We know that the date of the accident was 1938 (give or take a year). It probably happened in Eccles, in Manchester, but it could have happened when little Robin was in a cub scout camp. Our researchers have written to various registrars in Manchester, but without the exact date it is difficult to look up hundreds of registers. Our researcher has also contacted scout officials in Manchester but has received no reply.

The name is Robin Craddock from Eccles, Manchester, and also from North Wales. He died in some lake when he was eight years of age, and there was a Richard Jones, who we think was his uncle, connected with the accident. It would be so satisfying to tie this one up.

P.S: The luxury flats are now all let. All is quiet. This is the reason why we cannot give the name of the small town in North Wales where all this happened.

10   *The Anniversary Ghost*

I have never come across anniversary ghosts, the ones that do their own thing at regular times. Anne Boleyn is the best known, she who 'walks the Bloody Tower with her head tucked underneath her arm'. Presumably she does not amble every night. Perhaps annually, on her birthday or the anniversary of her execution. Portly gentlemen are reputed to walk down several manorial staircases once a year at the stroke of midnight.

Not so long ago I read of several people who had stood near a field in the English countryside when the whole area became alive with the sound of Spitfires and the raucous voices of many men as they rushed to carry out their wartime flying duties. The field, it was said, was an old RAF camp of the last war, and once a year, or perhaps once every ten or twenty-five years, it would become alive again and the ghosts of men of half a century ago would re-enact some most poignant hour of the camp's life.

I have wondered about this. Do dead men return to re-enact some pulsating scene from their earth lives? Or is it the act itself? Are there some incidents, some emotions, some loves, some hatreds, some fears, that people experience that are so strong, so powerful, that they cannot die, cannot be erased, and break out like daffodils through tarmacadam at regular intervals or anniversary dates?

A friend had this kind of experience many years ago. He had recently retired from his post as housemaster at a very reputable public school.

'I still think a great deal about it,' he said to me, 'but I'm blowed if I can solve the riddle at the end.'

I will tell you my friend's story, as he told it to me.

*

Peter Edwards, my friend, was eighteen when he won his state scholarship to Oxford. The headmaster of his grammar school, in a Welsh market town, declared a half-holiday to mark the honour conferred on his school.

The train journey to Oxford was Peter's first experience of leaving home. His scout – as a college servant is called – saw him, or sensed him, or whatever college scouts do, when he trudged through the main gate. He walked across the quad to greet him and to carry his baggage past the fountain to his rooms.

Peter had been allocated two rooms on the first floor. You walked up a narrow stone staircase to the little top landing. Room 16 was the first one on the landing. His scout opened the door and led him into a tiny, couldn't-swing-a-cat room. It had a small, black-leaded fireplace with a good fire burning in the open grate (the scout had seen to this), and it had a sink unit of a sort – at least, it had a sink and a cold-water tap. The door opposite the entrance door opened into an even smaller room. The scout pulled a rope handle, and a dilapidated, last-century bed detached itself painfully from the wall opposite the small leaded window. This was obviously his bedroom. The scout identified his tip and took his leave.

'Anything you want, sir, just call me, sir.'

'That evening,' said Peter, 'I felt desperately lonely and homesick.'

Later some of the students sauntered on to the quad. Peter looked down on them from his upstairs window. He couldn't make out what they were saying, but the voices were audible enough for him to know they were 'far back', speaking with the Oxford accent that he and his friends at the grammar had so often tried to mimic. He envied their clothes, the wide bags and the loud check jackets.

'It was only carpenters and plumbers who wore denim in those days,' said Peter.

Before very long the quadrangle seemed full of well-dressed young men, and Peter, the freshman, looked down on them through the translucent panes of his small, leaded window. They were probably regaling each other with tales of the long vac, exciting adventures in foreign lands, and love conquests of beautiful debutantes in the metropolis Peter had never visited.

'It must have been well after eleven o'clock before the quadrangle cleared,' said Peter, 'and it was only then that I made tracks for bed – my squeaky bed in the back bedroom.'

Peter unpacked his pyjamas that still carried a pleasant smell of Bradley's shop where his mother had bought all his college clothes.

It had become unnaturally quiet in that college precinct for 11.30 on a mild October evening.

Peter thought his mother would be in bed by now, but his father would still be up, reading one of his beloved Thackeray novels. He wondered if they missed him at home; they still had their other two children. It was strange how quiet it had become: there must be 300 students in the building. He had heard so much of the wild, all-night parties that students always had at college, and especially in Oxford. Those chaps in the quad half an hour ago couldn't possibly have all gone to bed, not at half past eleven!

His bed was cold and hard, and he shivered a little. His mother had warned him about sleeping in a damp bed. She had known of many Welsh ministers of religion, on preaching circuits, who had died through sleeping in a damp bed.

'I fell asleep,' said Peter, 'but looking back at it, it was an uneasy sleep. It wasn't that I was really cold, and there was nothing in the world to be afraid of, but I couldn't get hold of the slumber of home. I have no idea for how long I had been asleep in that bed when suddenly all Hell was let loose in the quadrangle below. High-pitched, excited voices were shouting and screaming, and the light of torches flashed on my leaded window.'

The hurrying of feet came nearer and nearer, and the voices were louder and harsher. Then heavy feet pounded up the stone staircase. There was shouting, yelling and cursing. They were trying to unlock the door of his living-room. Then one of them must have put his shoulder to it. From his bedroom sanctuary he heard the wood splintering, and then the door crashing on the linoleum floor of his small living-room. The voices penetrated through his bedroom door quite distinctly now. One of them was a rather effeminate voice, and it called, 'God Gawd! Gawd, who's got a bloody knife? Who's going to bloody cut him down?' And then a more guttural, deeper voice, possibly the voice of the one who had shattered his study door, 'Get him, Andrew! Hold him by the legs!'

Peter was sure that this was the freshman's rag and that he, Peter Edwards from Wales, was to be the first victim. But he had never thought of it being quite like this. It was supposed to be fun. His father had said: 'Students tend to lark about a little with freshmen you know, Pete. Just take it in good spirit, boy.'

God, this was no larking! He felt like Gordon of Khartoum.

An ashen-faced, quivering Peter opened his bedroom door to meet his tormentors and to submit to whatever sadistic initiation they demanded of him. But when he stepped clumsily into the study, it was empty, empty, perfectly still and quite undisturbed. He looked towards the study door. It was standing on its hinges and barred, just as it had been when he had gone to bed. He opened it very cautiously and stepped out on to the small landing – nothing. All he could hear was the faint sound of music, probably from the wireless set of the night porter's office down below.

I didn't ask Peter how he had slept the rest of the night. But he told me that at breakfast next morning one of the dons had thrown an almost rhetorical question at him: 'Slept well, I hope?' He had thrown all etiquette to the winds and broken all the rules of breakfast good manners by gabbling to him all the details of his ordeal the previous night.

'And it wasn't a dream or a nightmare, sir,' he said. 'I was fully awake. It was real. It happened.'

The don listened politely, munching his toast and nodding occasionally. Then he said, 'What room number are you, Mr Edwards?'

'Room 16,' said Peter.

'Ah, there lies the explanation, my boy!' said the philosophical sage. 'There have been two suicides in Room 16, Mr Edwards. Both were hangings. One was in the 1850s and the other, if I remember correctly, was somewhere around 1908. That's it, Mr Edwards, that explains it all, what? I mean, what you say you heard the men saying – "Who's got a bloody knife? Who's going to cut him down?" and all that. They weren't talking about you, Mr Edwards. It was a re-enactment, lad; it was the hanging all over again. Interesting, what?'

I told Peter I thought it a good story, but I couldn't see the riddle he had said puzzled him. The master's explanation of the event seemed quite plausible to me.

'The riddle, boyo,' said the public school master, reverting, under the influence of my Welsh accent, 'the riddle, boyo, is this. Which of the two suicides was being re-enacted in my room that night? If it was the 1850 hanging, it is, just as you say, a damn' good ghost story. Anne Boleyn with her head tucked underneath her arm, walking the Bloody Tower and all that. But what if it was the 1908 hanging that was re-enacted? This damn' thing happened to me in October 1950, just forty-two years after the second suicide. Damn it, man, some of the students, most of the students, who took part in that incident in 1908, would still be alive in 1950. The chappie with the effeminate voice could quite easily be a bishop in Western Australia, and the one who shouted, "Get him by the legs, Andrew" could be a GP in Llangefni.'

If it was the 1908 one, is it possible for living people to leave their bodies on one anniversary night – 'the bishop from Western Australia' and 'the GP from Llangefni'? Was it possible for them to come together for a few minutes to re-enact a macabre scene of the past, and at the moment when Peter opened his bedroom door and all had become quiet once again, had a bishop in Western Australia jerked his head back with a 'Sorry, my dear. I must have dozed off,' and had a GP at a p rty in Llangefni just at that same moment said to a vociferous patient, 'Sorry! You were saying?'

We in Wales are a psychic people. They do say that our roots are in the Far East, and I reminded Peter of an old Welsh saying: '*Gwell gweld ysbryd dyn marw nag ysbryd dyn byw*' – 'It's far less frightening to see the ghost of a dead person than to see the ghost of the living.'

11   *The Ghost That Changed House*

Ghost-sufferers normally refer themselves for help, but in this instance the call came from a community psychiatric nurse. She told me that she had a patient suffering from depression, but a funny kind of depression.

'I don't like to say too much over the phone,' she said. 'But I think, if you would call, you can do more for her than I can.'

Bethan James was an attractive young lady in her twenties. She and her two boys lived in a cottage of great character on the Isle of Anglesey; everything about it was spotless. She knew that I was coming and had very sensibly arranged for someone to take the boys swimming in Llangefni so that we could talk, because I still didn't know how I fitted into this depression situation.

She was a sensitive woman and got to the point straight away.

'I have been feeling depressed and edgy for a long time,' she said. 'I'm off my food, I smoke too much, I can't sleep at night, I have frequent bouts of crying and I am thoroughly miserable. I've been going to the doctor, and he's been giving me pills, but I don't seem to be getting any better.'

'How do you think I can help?' I asked her.

'It was the nurse's idea really – she said you know about ghosts and things.'

So we went back to the beginning.

Bethan had been a State Enrolled Nurse at Gwynedd Hospital. When she was twenty-two she met Brian at a disco in Beaumaris. They started going out together, and at the end of a year they became engaged. They found themselves in a funny situation, however, because Brian worked on the farm for his father. It wasn't even a farm – it was just a smallholding of thirty acres, but Brian's father also owned a large cattle-truck, and on at least three days a week he became a long-distance driver. This was the only life and the only job Brian knew, ploughing the thirty-acre land with a dilapidated tractor or riding cab with his father and helping to load and unload the animals. He couldn't remember his mother, for she had died when he was two, and rough old Owen James had been both father and mother to him ever since. But father didn't pay wages. There was always money available if he needed a new suit or a new pair of shoes or pocket money on Saturday night, but there was never a set wage. His father had always maintained that with wages the tax man took most of them, and anyway the smallholding and the business would all be Brian's one day.

That day came sooner than expected. Brian came home from evening class at the tech one night to find his father lying on the kitchen floor. He called the ambulance but Owen James was dead before he arrived in the hospital. The doctor said he had had a massive heart attack. He was only fifty-seven.

Beth and Brian had then decided that this was the time to get married. She would carry on with her nursing, and Brian felt sure that he could make a go of the farm and possibly double the animal carting trade.

They cleaned up the old home and spent hours together painting it and sprucing it up. They burned all the old carpets and replenished the house with good second-hand things from Morgan Evans' auction sales.

They got married in June, and within six months Beth was pregnant. It was that kind of pregnancy where everything went wrong. She was anaemic, her blood pressure soared, and nothing would bring it down. Her legs were swollen, and she had to lie in at the hospital for three months before Aled was born. So that was the end of her nursing career for a time and of her contributing to the family income. Brian worked hard on the smallholding but it was not a good year. One of the bullocks died a week before it was due for the market, vet's fees were heavy and somehow or other the carrier business didn't flourish as they had expected. There were other carters with much posher double-decker vans that could offer better rates than Brian could with his old Bedford.

Twelve months after Aled was born, almost to the day, Bryn came along.

Brian decided to give up the carrier business and took a job at a local factory in Llangefni. This would at least bring in a regular pay packet, and they could always rent the fields for grazing. With good management the four of them got by.

Then, one Saturday morning, Bethan and the little ones got up and realized that Daddy had got up before them and had left a note: 'Gone to Builth Wells. Back about 7 p.m.' He had taken the Bedford carrier.

He did arrive back at seven, as promised, but he was very pale and very agitated. It appeared that William Thomas had asked him to take some cows to Builth Wells, and as the money was good, he had decided to risk it. It had been all right going there, but on the way back the police had stopped him on the bridge, and now he was really in the soup. Beth couldn't understand why Brian was in the soup for taking his own van on a job, so he explained it to her. A month ago the tax had expired on the van, and he had cancelled the insurance, so now he would be in court for driving without tax and insurance and would have a fine of probably two or £300.

Then Beth, who had never been known to swear, had called him a bloody, bloody, bloody fool. She had told him that he was the stupidest, most slow-witted man she had ever met and that she and the children would have been better off if she had married Gwilym, the village idiot. She had then gone up to her bedroom and slammed the door. He went out to the yard. Ten minutes later she heard a shotgun go off; she rushed out. He was there by the paddock stile, and it didn't need a doctor to say that he was dead.

Bethan couldn't remember a great deal after that. Her parents had come, there was a funeral, although she couldn't remember much about it, and she had no idea what had happened to Aled and Bryn.

Her parents had come to the inquest with her. She had been asked to say what had happened on the evening on which Brian had died and she had been quite honest and had told the coroner all about his driving without tax and insurance and how she had given him a row. It was only in the coroner's court that she realized that, although she had said all those awful things to Brian, he hadn't said a word to her. The coroner asked, 'And what did Mr James say to all this?' and she said, 'He didn't say anything, I don't think.'

The police had given evidence as to how they had stopped Brian on the bridge and that it was probable that charges would have been pressed against him. But the police spokesman stressed that he had not seemed unduly worried. His employer was also called to answer questions.

'He was a good worker,' he said, 'and we all admired him for taking to factory life so well after years of a very different life on the farm.' Mr Redvers always thought of Brian as a very happy man – and no, he didn't think he had any worries.

The coroner had then summed up. He told Bethan not to brood about their little row. All married couples had these little rows, he said, and he felt that this had little to do with Brian's death and that she was not to blame herself. The police ballistics expert had given evidence that the gun that had killed Brian was of an unusual and obsolete German make. It had a faulty trigger, and it would appear that a sudden bang on the kitchen door would have been enough to set it off. The police were not prepared to release this gun until measures had been taken to repair it.

The coroner also said that at the time of his death Brian had had at his heels a very young, playful, undisciplined sheep dog, and the dog could have contributed to the accident.

'But,' said the coroner, 'the most telling fact in the case was the place of death.'

According to police evidence, Brian must have been killed whilst standing on the top rung of the paddock stile. People who committed suicide, said the coroner, chose the place of their demise carefully – a barn or a garage or some secluded place in the country, but never, in his nearly thirty years as a coroner, had he heard of anyone committing suicide on the top rung of a stile.

The jury brought in a verdict of accidental death, and once again the coroner told Beth not to dwell at all on their little tiff minutes before the accident. Beth was pleased about the verdict.

She missed Brian dreadfully and at times wondered if she could carry on. Five months after the funeral she arranged for a headstone to be placed on the grave. She and a neighbour went to see the stone, and it was very nice. She came home, gave the boys their tea and put them to bed. She herself went to bed a little after ten. She read for a bit before putting out the lights. Then there was a rap, rap on the chest of drawers, and Brian came and sat at the foot of the bed – and she could hear him.

The pace was now becoming too fast for me.

'Hold it, Beth,' I said. 'You said that Brian came and sat at the foot of the bed and you could hear him – did he speak to you?'

'No,' she said, 'but I could hear him whistling. It wasn't really a whistle. Every night when Brian came to bed, he would give a rap, rap on the chest of drawers with his finger-nails, and if he was embarrassed or had come in late or had had a couple of drinks with the lads, he would sort of whistle between his teeth, and I would know straight away he had a guilty conscience about something.'

'So you didn't see him that night?'

'No, but I knew he was there.'

Beth said it then became a pattern. He would come to the bedroom two or three nights a week. The rap, rap on the chest of drawers would make her jump sky-high, and the whistle would make her feel like lead inside.

'But you loved him,' I said. 'Why does his coming back make you unhappy?'

'I loved that man more than anything in the world. After he died I cried myself to sleep for weeks and weeks on end. I wanted to die, I missed him so much.' Then she began to cry. 'But now I am neither wife nor widow, and I wish he would stay away and leave us alone. He is dead and we are alive.'

She told me that her mother had a friend once who suffered from melancholia. She had never known what melancholia was until now, but every morning, after a visit from Brian, she would drag herself out of bed and go through her work like a leaded zombie. She was even too sad to cry, and she would be unable to shake herself free of this brooding until well in the afternoon.

At this stage her parents had persuaded her to move from the farmhouse to a little cottage that was for sale in the village near them. The proceeds from the sale of the farm were sufficient to buy the cottage and allow a very decent margin of profit that had been invested in a building society against a rainy day.

For three months she and Aled and Bryn were happy in their new cottage – and then Brian came again. One night there was the dreaded rap, rap on the chest of drawers, and the whistling, and she thought that the whistling denoted disapproval of their moving. It had gone on like that, and she had become more and more depressed. The doctor was giving her pills, but it wasn't pills she wanted, only someone to tell Brian that he was dead and that he should let those that were alive live their own lives.

I told her that I would have to ask my friend to join me in this, and would it be all right for me to tell him her story and to bring him along? She agreed willingly, but please could we do it quickly?

In this instance I told Elwyn everything I knew about Beth and Brian, how they met, how they got married, about the children, how really for their sakes he had taken on a factory job to get more money, and how he had hated it. I told him how Brian had inherited the truck and had tried to make a go of it and failed, how the police caught him without tax and insurance on the bridge, and about the accident, the inquest and the verdict of accidental death.

And I told him, too, of this unusual example of a ghost moving house. All the ghosts I had known seemed to have cat-like characteristics. Like cats, they seemed to have a greater affinity with the house than with the people living in it, and if the family moved to another house in another village, the ghost would remain and cohabit with the next set of tenants.

Elwyn was obviously interested in the ghost that moved house. This was perhaps a sign of great love, he thought, although in this case very misplaced.

When we got into Beth's tidy little cottage, Elwyn told her he knew all about her problem. She seemed quite at ease. She seemed to sense that Elwyn would be able to help her, and she was quite anxious to get on with it. I felt quite sure that this woman, unbeknown to herself, had very strong mediumistic qualities, and it was because of these that Brian was able to traipse, at will, across fields and hedges from the smallholding to this little cottage in the village.

The Beth–Brian story ended quite abruptly that night. Beth said to us in a quiet, unafraid voice: 'He's here now.'

Elwyn said: 'Yes, I know he is. He is standing in the hall.'

And I, as usual, could see no one and hear nothing.

Elwyn made the suggestion that I have heard him make many a time before.

'Beth,' he said, 'you have a choice. I think Brian wants to talk to you tonight. He can do this by using me to communicate or if you prefer it I can help you to become very relaxed, and in this relaxed state you and Brian could talk to each other directly.'

Some people are afraid of relaxing deeply at another person's command, but Beth agreed at once. She had obviously made up her mind that that night she was going to rid herself of something that had been worrying her for a very long time.

Then the countdown began.

'You are very tired. Your arms are getting heavy. Now relax. Fold your arms on your lap. Your eyes. Your eyelids are so heavy that they are like a heavy curtain: let them drop. Relax.'

In two minutes Beth was totally relaxed. No, she wasn't hypnotized, just in a lovely state of total relaxation, yet conscious of everything that was going on. I saw Elwyn was also relaxing and breathing differently, and I was left the odd man out in that little front parlour.

What happened next was just like what happens in our house, very often, when one of our children rings up the vicarage. My wife will answer, then one of the other children will pick up the second phone, and they have a sort of three-way conversation. On this night it was Brian who rang. Beth answered and Elwyn picked up the 'second phone'. I could hear only Beth's side of the conversation.

'Yes, yes, of course I love you,' she was saying. 'Yes, honest, Bri. I have always loved you and I still do. Of course you weren't selfish. Don't blame yourself, dear. No, Bri, please, I don't want to hear about that. Please, Bri, don't tell me. I knew it wasn't an accident. But I was glad the coroner said it was. All right, I will listen then.' There followed minutes when I heard nothing. Then just a simple: Thank you, Bri,' and the spiritual phone was put down.

Elwyn said: 'Now, Beth, you know it was no accident.'

Beth said, 'I have always known, really.'

It appeared that, as soon as Brian had died, he had regretted his foolish act and was blaming himself for having been so selfish, leaving Beth and the boys to fend for themselves. He had come back, time and again, to say to Beth how sorry he was. Although he had sat on the edge of her bed and shouted his love for her, and his shame for letting her down, he knew she had not heard him. But this night contact had been made.

I felt on this occasion that in some way I had been neglected and ignored! Beth and Elwyn had had their secret telephone, and I had had to be content with but one part of the conversation.

I said to her: 'Well, I hope you made it quite clear that you now wish to be left alone to lead your own life.'

Both Beth and Elwyn looked quite pitifully at me.

'He won't be back,' said Beth. 'I know it's right this time. I feel it inside me.'

'No. We can go home now,' said Elwyn.

The next day I went to see a friend in hospital. She had had a major operation two years before. The trouble had recurred and she had had to have a second and a third operation. Then a month ago the surgeon had said there was a blockage, a stone or a lesion, and she would have to go in for her fourth big operation. I was almost afraid of what I was going to see when I turned into her ward. But there she was, sitting up in bed, smiling.

'How was it?' I asked.

'Great,' she said. 'I know he's got it right this time. I feel it inside me.'

I thought to myself: Beth said that last night.

It had all been so complete. Elwyn had been so professional, and Bethan so sensible. There was no need for further research, no questions remained unanswered. This was very different from the hospital experience that was to follow.

12 The Last Will and Testament

This story is not a ghost story, but it is about an incident that has intrigued me for many years. It happened in the old Caernarfon and Anglesey Hospital in Bangor, and it happened at one of those times when the old hospital became chock-a-block full and they had to have beds set up in corridors. I had a very dear parishioner dying in hospital that night, and I had been keeping her company until her son could arrive from Birmingham.

It was a nice summer evening, and it must have been about 9.30 when I eventually took my leave. I said goodnight to the sister and walked down the long corridor, nodding and exchanging greetings with the occupants of the corridor beds. I was just about to reach the door when one of the patients called out to me: 'Excuse me,' he said. 'Are you a minister of religion?'

I told him I was the vicar of Llandegai. The patient sat bolt upright in bed. He propped his two pillows deftly against the wall behind him and beckoned me to sit on the chair by his bed.

'I wonder if you can do me a favour, Reverend?' he said, and I had a feeling from the way he asked his question that I was going to be sitting on this little chair, in the corridor of the C & A Hospital, for a long time.

My interceptor was a clean-shaven, florid-looking gentleman in his mid-sixties, with white hair, a shining bald patch and clean, well-kept hands holding the bedclothes.

'I wonder if you would make my will for me, Reverend? I've got paper in my locker and a biro.'

'Fine,' I said. 'It's a wise thing to make a will. I'll come back tomorrow and have a chat with you about it.'

'But I don't want to do it tomorrow,' said the florid

gentleman. 'I want to do it tonight.'

Then, in a tone that was slow and deliberate, in a way that suggested that he didn't want to be misunderstood or to antagonize his benefactor-designate, he proceeded to tell me about his predicament.

He was John Pritchard and he farmed two large farms on Anglesey. He lived on one, and his farm manager lived on the other. He and his wife had no children, but for the past nineteen years his wife's sister had lived with them on the farm. The Lord had been good to them: they had flourished and, he told me with a wink, he had 'a nice packet put away'. He went on to explain why he was so anxious to make his will.

'I know,' he said, 'that if I die intestate, my wife Ann will get the lot. There will be some bother with solicitors and things,' he said, 'but in the end she will get the lot.'

'And that is not what you want?' I said.

'Well, yes,' said Farmer Pritchard, 'that would be all right. I know she would share with her sister, Margaret. I mean, Margaret would be all right, too. But it's not the same.'

John Pritchard felt that Margaret, his sister-in-law, had worked just as hard on the farm as his wife, Ann, and himself, and that she had every right to her own share of the proceeds.

'My wife and her get on well together,' said the old man. 'Ann won't see her go short, but I want her to have her own share. It isn't right for her to have to go and ask for money to go on holiday or buy a hat. So,' he said, 'will you make my will tonight, please?'

'No,' I said, 'I won't. But I will bring a solicitor along tomorrow.'

It was then that John Pritchard exploded.

'But I won't be here tomorrow. I am going to die tonight.'

I felt sorry for the old man. He was so determined and, after all, making a will doesn't take long. At least the wills that parsons are usually asked to draw up don't take long – 'the clock to my son William, the dresser to my daughter May, and the rocking chair to my granddaughter Sandra'. My commission that night in the C & A was different. We were going to dispose of two farms and a thousand acres of land, plus a nice packet in the bank, and I thought it called for someone more knowledgeable than a village parson, writing on a piece of paper from the hospital locker.

'I promise you I will be back tomorrow morning,' I said, 'and I will have a solicitor with me.'

Then the old man started pleading with me.

'Please, please, Reverend,' he said, clutching my arm. 'Please believe me when I tell you that I won't be here tomorrow. I shall be dead.' There were tears welling up in his eyes.

He looked so healthy there in his corridor bed, and his grip on my arm was like a clamp. In any case, hospital sisters know what they're doing. Had there been the slightest chance of his dying in the night, the sister would have found some good reason for moving his bed from the public corridor. There might be emergencies in which hospital authorities set up beds in the public corridors, but no way, I thought to myself, would hospital authorities allow people to die in public corridors.

I wrenched my arm free of the old man's grip.

'Just wait a minute,' I said. 'I will just go and have a word with sister about this.' I fled to sister's office and told her all about it.

'Old John Pritchard, you mean?' she said. 'The one with the white hair, in the bed by the door in the corridor?'

'Yes,' I told her. 'He tells me he knows he's going to die during the night and that he won't be here in the morning.'

'Well, he'd better be,' said sister, 'because in the morning doctor is doing his rounds and in the afternoon John P. will be on his way home to his cows and his sheep in Anglesey. You go home this way,' sister said to me, 'and I will go and have a chat with the old boy – take him a cuppa. He's only had a rupture operation anyway.'

It was after ten by the time I got home, and all the time I wondered whether I had done the right thing. So I rang the hospital chaplain and told him all about it and that I wasn't sure.

'I'll pop down and see him,' said the chaplain.

An hour later he rang me back and told me he had had exactly the same treatment. It had been 'Help me because I'm going to die.'

'Anyway,' said the chaplain, 'I promised him a solicitor

first thing in the morning, so you needn't bother. I'll take over from here.'

I felt a lot easier going to bed knowing the buck now lay on somebody else's desk.

Eight o'clock the following morning the telephone rang. It was the hospital chaplain. He just said: 'Old John Pritchard had a massive heart attack in the middle of the night and died at five o'clock this morning.'

13   A Ghost That Was Not a Ghost

Bob and Doris Evans were probably in their late sixties when they came to retire to our village. They had kept their own little corner shop somewhere on Merseyside, and by sheer hard work, long hours and being kind and pleasant, they had built up a good business and had made enough money to retire to North Wales. Many elderly couples do this. They seem to want to come back to where they enjoyed a blissful honeymoon, nearly half a century ago, or spent a holiday of youth and fantasized about it over the years. Very often it doesn't work out. It is difficult for a couple in their sixties to make new friends in a new part of the country. When one dies, the other is left a lonely sojourner in a foreign land.

Bob and Doris weren't like this. He was an expert gardener who always managed to grow, from seed, far more lettuce, cabbage and bean plants than he had room for in his own garden, and he was an expert at taking cuttings. Other gardeners always seemed to congregate around Beech Cottage. Their wives got to know Doris when they called with a few Welsh cakes and to say 'thank you' for Bob's cuttings.

Bob was in his eighties when he had to go to hospital for an operation. It was something quite normal – the removal of a prostate gland or some such elderly ailment. Doris packed his bag for him, and a neighbour ran him into the hospital and saw him safely into the surgical ward. Two days later Bob had his operation and was fine – no complications whatsoever. The same day, when a neighbour called in to see Doris, she found her sitting in her chair – and she was dead. She had a half-drunk cup of tea on the table beside her, and the radio was still on, but the neighbour knew before she phoned the doctor that Doris was dead.

When you break bad news to people, they never react as television producers imagine they do. They don't scream or collapse in a limp heap on to the furniture. Elderly people in particular have a dignified way of receiving bad news. I told Bob that I had bad news for him. I told him it was about Doris. I explained to him that the doctor was with me at the bedside because of the bad news, and Bob still waited patiently, so I said,

'I'm afraid Doris is dead, Bob.'

His reply was: 'Oh! poor old Doris! How did it happen?'

I told him how the neighbour had found her and that the doctor had said there would have to be a post-mortem and we didn't know, especially with him being in hospital, when we could arrange the funeral. Bob understood about the post-mortem but he asked me if I would arrange the funeral for him. Doris had always said she wanted cremation, and Bob would like the service to go ahead as soon as possible and not to wait for him to be discharged from hospital.

I went to see him in hospital several times to tell him about the post-mortem report and to ask him about flower arrangement for the funeral and if there were any special hymns he thought Doris would have liked. Every time I called, he would have written out little notes and instructions, names of family and friends who should be notified, and a special notice for friends on Merseyside. On the evening of the funeral I went to the hospital to report and to give him a list of all those present and notes of sympathy from friends. I took a prayer book with me to show him what lesson I had read, and what psalm had been used – and the hymns. Bob was very grateful, and pleased that Doris had had a nice funeral.

The nurses all felt that the shock of Doris's death would come later, and they kept Bob in an extra week to make sure that he would be all right going back to an empty house. It had been arranged that a home help would call three times a week, and he would have Meals on Wheels the two working days when she didn't call. The neighbours would keep an eye on him at weekends. Bob got on fine, and within a couple of months he was back in the garden and pottering in the greenhouse. He was obviously missing Doris, and his therapy was endless talk about her, how she used to love ironing and how she used to bake cakes every Wednesday, and the kind of books she liked to read – the neighbours would listen because talk was Bob's way of casting away his grief.

Two or three months elapsed. The villagers agreed that Bob had got over his bereavement well. He had driven himself once or twice to town in his own car, and he was managing so well in the house that Social Services had withdrawn the home help. The social worker had explained to Bob that there were others who needed her more, and he had agreed.

Doris had been dead about six months when I called to see Bob one morning as I was coming home from church. He was working in the garden and when he saw me, he asked if I would pop in. He wanted my advice about something. I walked in and Bob took his wellies off, washed his hands in the kitchen sink and filled the kettle for a cuppa. Then I noticed that he seemed a little bit agitated. He picked up an envelope and I noticed his hands were shaking as he handed me the contents. It was a red reminder notice that he had not paid his water rates.

'That came yesterday,' he said. 'Now let me show you the original one.' He gave it to me and then he said, 'Is that one receipted, do you think?'

I looked at it and told him that it wasn't a receipt, it was a bill, and as far as I could see, it hadn't been paid. At this poor old Bob got quite agitated.

'But it has been paid, Vicar,' he said. 'I went to the office myself and I handed in the money over the counter. I had been for my pension that day and I crossed the road to the town hall and paid it.'

'But Bob, if you had paid it, you would have had a receipt stamp,' I said.

'Look, Vicar,' said Bob, 'I am not going to argue about this. I tell you that bill is paid. If it was just me saying it, I could be wrong. I do forget a lot of things these days, but it is not just me saying it. I asked Doris last night, and Doris told me that it was definitely paid. She remembered me paying it.'

'Bob, when did Doris tell you you had paid the bill?' I asked.

'Last night,' he said. 'She was sitting in that chair that you are sitting in now, and I showed her this red reminder that had come and she said, "But you've paid it, Bob," and she reminded me that it had been on the same day I drew my pension from the post office.'

At this point in the conversation the vicar cleared his throat and got down to some corrective therapy.

'Let's work this one out quietly together, Bob,' I said. 'You remember, six months ago, you went to hospital for your operation?'

'Yes.'

'And do you remember that when you had been there only a couple of days I came to see you and brought you very bad news?'

'Yes,' said Bob.

'I told you that Doris had died suddenly.'

'Yes.'

'And I came again and told you about the cremation, Doris's cremation.'

'Yes.'

'So, Bob, you will have to get hold of yourself. Doris is dead, Bob. She is not coming back, Bob. One day you will be together again, but not now.'

Bob looked me straight in the eye for a long time.

'When you came to hospital to tell me that Doris was dead, I accepted what you said as a fact. When you told me about her funeral in the crematorium, I accepted it as a fact.' And, with a quiver in his voice, he added, 'So why, Vicar, can't you accept it when I say to you that I asked Doris last night, when she was sitting in that chair you're sitting in now, if I had paid the water rates bill and she told me I had?'

There was no answer to that question.

14   *The Ghost of a Living Man*

It seems odd, when one writes in English, to speak of the ghost of a living person, in Welsh, *ysbryd dyn byw* sounds perfectly normal. Many people have told me they have seen what appeared to be ghosts only to meet them in real life months later.

We had rather an unnerving experience of this kind of thing in the vicarage some years ago. My eldest son, who was working in Manchester as a trainee reporter, was home for a few days leave. He had been shopping in Bangor and came into the house as everyone else does, through the front door. His schoolgirl sister, Felicity, just gaped at him.

'How did you come here?' she asked.

'I've just been to Bangor,' he answered, 'and now I'm coming back again. OK?'

But Felicity was really agitated. 'You can't have been in Bangor,' she said. 'I just walked past you this second, standing in the dining-room.' And then she added, 'And you had different clothes on in the dining-room. You were wearing your yellow waistcoat.'

The embroidered yellow waistcoat had been Mark's Christmas present from his mother, and he used to wear it with great pride. He assured us that on that day the embroidered yellow waistcoat was hanging in the wardrobe of his lodgings in Manchester. But Felicity was adamant.

The incident passed and was never mentioned again, but we were all very relieved, a couple of years later, when my son told us that the embroidered yellow waistcoat had become too tight for him and he had passed it on to Oxfam. All this was very nearly twenty years ago.

It was years later that I heard the stories told of Padre Pio, who never left his Italian monastery but frequently appeared in the cottages that surrounded the monastery, to give help to the poor, sick and needy. Had I known about Padre Pio earlier, perhaps the yellow waistcoat would not have seemed such an omen of disaster to my wife and me.

Engineers today are able to connect 'governors' to car engines and electric motors. These governors prevent the engine from travelling at more than a specified speed, or the electric motor from generating too high a current of electricity. I often think that the human mind, whilst on this earth, has such a governor. A person is able to see quite clearly his present surroundings and environment; he is able to look back and remember quite vividly what has gone before, but the governor prevents him from looking forward to what is to be. Sometimes I think this governor slips, and a person may have a quick glimpse into a scene or a place of the future – a glimpse, perhaps, of a little tea-shop in a cobbled lane in Amsterdam. Four years later, standing in a cobbled lane in Amsterdam, that person is able to say to a companion: 'I have a feeling that I have been here before, and if I remember rightly, there should be a nice little tea-shop just around the corner.'

Gypsies and other clairvoyants can slip the governor off at will, and many of them can see very clearly into the future. I know a lady who was neither gypsy nor clairvoyant and yet under great stress managed for a matter of moments to let her governor slip.

When I first came to Bangor to live, I came to know a lovely old couple, Councillor and Mrs William Pritchard. They kept the sub-post office. She looked after the shop – a cross between a grocery/newsagent/general ironmongery/gift shop, and he, dressed always in his flat cap and a dark grey overall coat, looked after the affairs of the Royal Mail in the furthest corner of the premises, marked off by a mahogany counter and a metal grille. The sub-post office/shop was their front parlour. During slack periods of the day, Mrs Pritchard would slip into the house to prepare a meal, and sometimes the councillor would go in and warm his hands by the kitchen fire, but always there would be one person on stand-by duty. If a shop customer entered, the postmaster from behind his grille would call out to the kitchen, 'Shop, please, Mrs

Pritchard,' and if a stamp or pension-book customer came, Mrs Pritchard would not dare cross the mahogany divide to the post office – she would call the postmaster to serve. It was actually a very busy little sub-post office. Many of the city's pensioners would walk past 'the general' to cash their pension books with Pritchard the Post. It was possible to draw one's pension here and report a neighbour's clogged drains at the same time.

Councillor and Mrs Pritchard had one son, Hefin. He had done well at school, but the summer he had done his 'A' levels, war had broken out and he had joined the RAF. He was now a pilot officer/navigator and had clocked several trips over Germany. His parents hated it and lived in dread throughout their waking hours. But for the last six months Hefin had been in Canada. He was an instructor, and they were so relieved that he was there and not flying over Germany.

It was one cold night in late November that Elizabeth Pritchard woke up, hot and trembling, and turned to wake her husband.

'Wake up, William! Oh, William! Our Hefin has had an awful accident. I'm afraid he's dead, William.'

'How do you know, Lisa *bach*?' asked half-awake William.

'I've seen it, William,' she said. 'I saw every minute of it.'

'Lisa *bach*, you've just had an awful dream,' William said. 'I'll go downstairs and make us both a cup of tea, and perhaps if you take an aspirin you'll be able to go back to sleep.'

When he came back with the tea, Elizabeth was much calmer, and by the time she had drunk her tea, the trembling had gone, but she was still very pale and there was a sort of wild, frightened look in her eyes.

'William,' she said, 'I know you think I have had a dream, a nightmare, but it wasn't a dream, William, it's real. Our Hefin has had a dreadful accident. He is very badly injured, but he was alive when I left him ...'

'Lisa *bach*,' said William, 'what do you mean when you left him? You have been in bed all night, *cariad*, and in the day ...'

'Listen to me, William,' said Elizabeth again. 'I know I was in bed, and I heard Hefin calling, "Mam! Mam!" to me, and there was an awful storm – a blizzard. I could hardly see my hand in front of my face, and then I heard the woo-woo-woo noise those old bomber planes make, and I could see it, a black shape against the snow, and I knew it was Hefin's plane flying in this fierce blizzard. It was flying very low and then it crashed, William. Our Hefin's plane crashed into that mountain.'

William tried to persuade her once again that it was a dream.

'I saw it, William. The nose of the old thing had plunged into the snow, and it was hanging there and it was all quiet. I waited to see if Hefin, or any of the men, would come out but nothing happened. It was now so very quiet, and it had even stopped snowing. There was a thin wisp of smoke coming from underneath the left wing of the plane. After waiting a bit, I opened the door of the plane.'

'Oh, *cariad bach*!' said William. 'Opened the door of the plane? Fair play, Lisa. You must know now that it was just a bad dream. You couldn't open the door of a plane.'

'I opened the door, William, and I went inside. There were five men in that plane. Three were in the front, where it had hit the mountain. They were dead. There was another one in the back. Poor boy, he had been very nearly cut in half, and he was dead. Then lying on the floor of the plane, face down, was our Hefin. He had hit his head, and there was a lot of blood, and his leg was twisted right round, as if it didn't belong to him, and oh! William, I think little Hefin was dead too, and nobody will be able to find them in all that snow.

'And William,' she said firmly, 'it wasn't a dream – don't you say it was a dream because I saw it all with my own eyes.'

The next day Councillor Pritchard took sole charge of the front parlour business. He had persuaded Elizabeth to have a lie-in that day, and when customers came to the shop he would come out from behind the grille to serve them with their tea and sugar without once calling out to the kitchen, 'Shop, Mrs Pritchard, please.'

Hefin sent them a letter every week telling them all about his work training young flyers in Canada, but this week no letter came. William tried to comfort Elizabeth that perhaps it was because of the convoy. The Germans often battered British convoys, and many ships were lost.

It was three weeks before a letter did arrive. Hefin was fine. He had been moved to another base in Canada, and his promotion to flight lieutenant had come through. The new place was nicer, and he had been taken off flying duties for a bit. There was one snag though: because of this move, his leave would now be postponed and he probably would not come home for six months. He was safe, that was the main thing, and William didn't even think of reminding Lisa that he had told her all the time that it was a dream.

Everyone who came to the shop would ask, 'How's Hefin?' and they would tell their customers that he was still in Canada, he'd been promoted but was not flying any more, just teaching, and they were so pleased that he was not flying.

When the great day came, they hired a taxi to take them to Bangor station. Hefin had written to say that he would arrive on the 3.45 p.m. train. They were on Platform 3 in very good time, and they had told the taxi to wait. They saw the train emerging from the tunnel and slowing down before it arrived on Platform 3. Before the train had stopped even, doors were being flung open, and young soldiers and girls in uniform were jumping out into the arms of people on the platform who had come to meet them. But there was no sign of Hefin. The two porters were already slamming the carriage doors shut again when William Pritchard saw an airman's rucksack being thrown out of the train window, followed by a single crutch. Then the door opened, one leg stretched out onto the platform and then came Hefin, leaning heavily on the other crutch and waving to them. The old people rushed up to him. Hefin was wounded but he was alive and he was home.

No one mentioned the injury or the crutches on the way home. Hefin wanted to know about Harriet the cat and whether they were all getting enough to eat on their rations and if old James Jones was still alive.

It was after tea that William Pritchard said to him, 'I see you've been wounded, lad.'

Hefin told them all about it. They were on a training trip over Alaska, five of them in the plane, when they flew right into a blizzard. They were flying low, trying to get a bearing, when they crashed into a mountain. Fortunately another plane was following, its crew were able to give map readings of their last position when they returned to base, and rescue planes had found them. Hefin told them that four of the crew had died instantly on impact; he himself was still unconscious when they found him and had been bleeding profusely from a head wound, and his leg had been shattered.

He told them, 'I didn't want you to worry. There was nothing you could have done anyway, so I wrote those silly letters to you about being posted to another base – being off flying, and leave cancelled for six months, and things. That was because the MO told me I would not be fit to travel for six months.

'But,' he said, 'they've made a lovely job of my leg. I had dozens of ops, and at each one the surgeon would do a jigsaw with my splintered bones.'

'Can you remember when this happened?' his father asked him, but before Hefin could answer, Elizabeth Pritchard said, 'It was at one o'clock in the morning on Thursday 17 November last year.'

An easy explanation would be to say that this was a wonderful demonstration of waking telepathy. A terrified flight lieutenant's crying out for his mother in that awful blizzard in Alaska and then able, through unconsciousness, to transmit to her pictures of his predicament that were so vivid that he had them imprinted so clearly on her mind. But this kind of explanation cannot be the right one. Hefin had never seen the plane plunging into the mountain, but his mother had. Hefin had not seen the bodies of his four dead comrades inside the plane, for he was still unconscious when his rescuers took him out of the plane – he only knew of their death because others had told him days later. And there was that wisp of smoke from underneath the left wing. Hefin knew nothing at all about that. Probably not even the rescuers knew about that. Only Elizabeth Pritchard knew about that little bit of smoke because she was the only one who had seen it.

Hefin had never transmitted any pictures to his mother. She had heard his cry, and she had got out of her bed in the sub-post office in Bangor, and she had travelled all the way to Alaska and had seen the whole awful thing for herself before coming back to her body to tell William all about it and to drink his tea.

15   The Churchyard Ghost

For many years I have been traipsing around the countryside sorting out other people's ghosts. It was only this year that I found that I had my own ghost in Llandegai – and, pertinently enough, in the churchyard.

Llandegai is possibly one of the smallest parishes in Britain. It was carved out especially for me when I was appointed to carry out social work in the diocese. The bishop, in his wisdom, was reducing my parish priest workload to the minimum whilst allowing me an altar access for all my diocesan problems.

We know that our present church is the third Christian church in the parish, and we know the sites of the other two. Our first church – we know its location – was built by St Gai in 555 or thereabouts, long before St Augustine came from Rome to preach. The parish consists of a model village (pop.200) just at the junction of the A5/A55, and a beautiful fourteenth-century church. Towering over the village is the pseudo-Gothic Penrhyn Castle, seat of the Penrhyn family, and one of the show-places of the National Trust. Roads from the village reach to the forests and gardens of Penrhyn Park, and for centuries castle and village have been closely linked together – through good days and bad.

It came as a great shock to me when I was told that I had a ghost in my churchyard, and I wasn't just told once about my ghost: I was told nineteen times in nineteen letters that arrived by the same day's post. The postman delivered the package on a Tuesday morning. I opened it and found it contained nineteen letters from pupils of Standard III, Ysgol Glancegin, of the Maesgeirchen estate that borders our village.

Ghost calls in the past had been from one individual or two

ysgol glancegin
maesgeirchen
Bangor
Gwynedd
North wales
115715t
may 5th 1989

Dear Vicar
We have been studying the family of walter
Speed. Walter Speed was the head gardener of penrhyn
gardens. Walter Speed had Fourteen children and he had
the Queen victoria gold medal for one of the sixty
best gardeners. when we went to Llandegai we
Found the name David white in the visitors
book. So there is a weird mystery! why would a man
come to see a little girl's grave who had died a
hundred years ago. And what's strange is that he put
down in the visitors book that he had seen
Rosa speed. But how could he have seen Rosa, because
Rosa had died over a hundred years ago. So how
could have seen or known her?
I think his writing is very tidy for a tramp. we do
not know how he had seen Rosa speed. Could you
help is please?
Your's
Sincerley
Dawn murray
age 10

or three persons at the most, but here was a cry for help from nineteen young children. On my way to the office I called at Glancegin School. I was welcomed by the headmaster, who was obviously expecting me and escorted me to Standard III and introduced me to the teacher, Mr Robert Wyn.

It was Mr Wyn who got down to explaining to me what it was all about. He had suggested to the class that it might be a good idea to start an out-of-doors historical project, and the class had agreed. (The school in Maesgeirchen is open-plan, and it seemed also to be a very democratic school.) Mr Wyn had then asked, 'A project on what?' The school is on a hill overlooking Penrhyn Park, the castle towers seem level with its playground, and it seemed natural that the choice should be some project about Penrhyn Castle. The democracy of Standard III, however, ruled that the project should not be about the main family but about the man who had made Penrhyn Gardens one of the three best gardens in Britain. The project was about Walter Speed and his large family.

In the middle of the last century Lord Penrhyn, the slate baron, was supplying slates for the roofs of the world and was one of the richest people in the country when he advertised for a head gardener in 1863. A young gardener from Ireland, aged twenty-eight, applied for the job, and he was to retain that position until he died aged eighty-six in 1921. That man was Walter Speed.

During Walter Speed's stewardship Penrhyn Gardens grew in reputation throughout the land. It was said that in his time there were three outstandingly beautiful gardens in Britain: the gardens of the Earl of Devonshire, the gardens of the Duke of Westminster, the gardens of Baron Penrhyn of Llandegai. Men came from afar to be taught their horticulture by this young gardener from Ireland. He was a hard taskmaster, but his apprentices had little difficulty in obtaining senior posts in the best gardens, and many of his pupils became curators of royal gardens.

Mr Wyn told me all this, and as he spoke of Walter Speed there was the hero-worship look in the eyes of all the nineteen members of the project team. It seemed to say, 'You can have your Ian Rush or your Boris Becker or your Paul Newman. Give us Walter Speed every time.'

Walter Speed, they told me, had married Charlotte and

The Family Tree of the Speeds

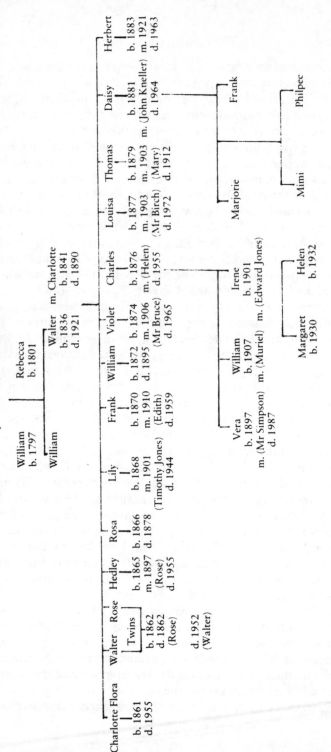

Simon McElligott

they had had fourteen children. The school produced a family tree and had it pinned on the wall.

The pupils of Standard III rattled off the Speed Table of Affinities quicker than most recited the two-times-table. To them the Speed family was an open book, and they all took such great pride in the fact that their Mr Speed had been amongst the chosen few to receive the VMH, Queen Victoria's gold medal for his service to horticulture.

The project was going well. The previous week they had all gone to Llandegai church to look at the pews in which Mr and Mrs Walter Speed and their maidservant used to sit. Simon McElligot stayed in the back and was browsing through the visitors' book in the baptistry. Then there was a shout from Simon: 'Mr Wyn! Mr Wyn! Come and see what I have found! Quick! It's about Rosa!'

There was apparently a stampede towards the back. Simon showed them a peculiar entry in the book. It was one for the previous year. The visitors' book is set in columns: date, name, address, remarks. This entry gave a date and the name David White, address as 'travelling', and in the remarks column it said, for all to see, 'Come to visit my little Rosa Speed.' There were other entries, and one with just the word 'Rosa!', which it seemed to suggest that on his last visit David White and Rosa had failed to meet.

The mystery had now been expounded. David White, who called himself a traveller and who possessed good, adult writing, had visited Llandegai church on several occasions. His messages on the church register more than suggested that he was coming to the church, and churchyard, just to meet little Rosa Speed. If this Rosa Speed was the Rosa the children knew, a daughter of Walter Speed, she would have died on 3 September 1878, aged eleven years ten months, and her body would have been buried under the large yew tree in the churchyard.

'What do you make of it,' asked Mr Wyn, 'that a man says that in your churchyard he can meet a child that has been dead for 111 years?'

As 'Sir' came to the end of his narration and his question, I could feel the eyes of Standard III almost willing me to give any kind of explanation for this peculiar friendship. I had to tell them that I knew of Walter Speed, I had actually met two of his daughters and I knew one of his granddaughters very well, but that I knew nothing of Rosa or this travelling person, David White. I promised I would make enquiries.

To add to the mystery, one of the girls told me that her father had met an old man from Llandegai and had told him the story of David White and Rosa, and the old man had said, 'It's funny you should say that. Sometime last summer, when I was taking flowers for my wife's grave, I saw a man dressed like a tramp, and he went into the church. When, after half an hour, he hadn't come out again, I went in. I saw the tramp kneeling by the altar, and he was praying; about ten minutes later he left. I went to close the church door after him, and I happened to look at the visitors' book. There was only one entry for that day, and it was for David White – it must have been him.' The old man also remembered that he had good handwriting for a tramp.

Standard III was determined to solve the mystery, so I did what I have done several times before: I sold the mystery to an S4C television film team. They liked it. They spent the morning filming the children at work on their project in school, and they invited me to join them for the afternoon filming session in the churchyard.

Things went well. I couldn't tell who was the more excited, 'Sir' or Standard III. They had been placed, two by two, behind their teacher, ready to enter the church, when camera 2, in the church porch, suffered a technical hitch, and I could see that the break was causing tension and that the excitement so essential to the film was beginning to drain from the children's expressions. To re-ignite interest and get them to relax again, I called out to them from the sidelines, 'Do you really want to know who this David White is? Shall I tell you?'

Eyes lit up and there was a chorus of, 'Yes, please tell us. Please.'

So, I told them: 'Well, David White is me really. I knew you were doing this project, so to play a trick on you I put on old clothes and disguised myself and signed the register.'

I thought this confession would be followed by a loud guffaw, but it wasn't, and Mr Wyn turned to me and said, 'What you say is not so funny, you know. We have regular seminars about this thing and we always ask the question,

has anyone any ideas at all who this David White could be? And last week,' said Mr Wyn, 'Richard Jones came out with this idea. Tell him what you said, Richard.'

'I said, I wondered if it was the vicar playing a trick on us.'

The film producer had decided that he would close the short magazine film by having me explain this peculiar phenomenon to the viewers. When I told him I hadn't a clue about this happening, I think this rather put him out, and he reminded me that I was the well-known ghost man in North Wales – 'Aelwyn the Ghost', as it were, and if I couldn't explain it, who could? In defence of my title and my reputation, I did tell him that the whole thing didn't really amaze me very much. I told him that I had friends who had frequent contacts, and chats, with people who had been dead a long time and that I felt sure that if anyone did find the elusive David White, he would find that he was a medium too.

'Sir', Standard III and I had a most exciting day out.

If you visit Llandegai church, you will find a note pasted on the table that holds the visitors' book. It reads,

Dear David White
If you come again to see Rosa Speed, we want you to know there are others also that love Rosa. Please leave a message that we can give to the pupils of Standard III, Ysgol Glancegin.

Aelwyn Roberts
Vicar

August and October are his usual times. We will keep our fingers crossed.

16   The Ghost of the Unmarried Mother

It started when a very worried lady called to see me at the vicarage. She lived in a neighbouring village, and she came because she and her husband were being troubled by a ghost.

Neither of them had seen anything or anybody. There had been no bangings or chain-rattling, but there was someone or something in their house. It had become a cold house, and it had become a gloomy house. Their children were grown up and married and there were just the two of them living there. And they both hated it because, over the past few years, it had become 'a house of depression'. When she and her husband went out to meet friends or to a concert or to visit their grandchildren, they would be happy, but always the joy and the laughter would dry up when they turned the key in their front door.

I was fed up with ghosts, and I didn't want to go. In any case, nests when the chicks had flown did very often become empty and cheerless. This couple now faced what many other couples had to face, and what my wife and I would one day have to face when the last of our six children left home.

I asked my visitor if there was any specific place in the house that was colder or gloomier than another, and she said: 'Yes, it is our bedroom at the top of the stairs. Whatever it is seems to be crouching near our bedroom door.'

The lazy ghostbuster then gave out his armchair remedy for haunting: 'Go home,' I said to the poor lady, 'and place a cross or a crucifix on your bedroom wall. Say a little prayer as you enter the room.' I also taught this good Nonconformist lady to make the sign of the cross and then, shame on me, I saw her out and into her car.

Within a month she was back. This time not just to tell me her story but to plead. Things had become worse, much worse, and now neither she nor her husband could face going up the stairs. They now slept downstairs, and the ghost had taken over the first floor.

I made my arrangements with Elwyn, and we agreed to visit the house the following Thursday evening.

I remember a little incident connected with this venture. My daughter Bridget had just graduated as a psychologist and asked if she could come along. I rang Elwyn to see if he minded. His reply was: 'I was just going to ring you to ask if you would mind if I brought *my* daughter with me. She too has just graduated in psychology at Swansea.'

So off we went at about seven o'clock on a summer's evening, Elwyn and I and the two girls. When we got to the house, Elwyn's sensitivity or whatever it is that tells him there is a ghost about – marched him straight up the stairs and into the bedroom right at the top of the landing. He then retreated back to the landing.

'This is where we will stay,' he said. 'The atmosphere is stronger here than anywhere else in the house.'

So we all made ourselves as comfortable as we could on the landing outside the bedroom door.

Mrs Parry, our hostess, told us: 'The vicar called this afternoon, and I told him that Mr Elwyn Roberts and the vicar of Llandegai were coming this evening. He asked if he could walk around the house.'

Apparently, as he was leaving, he told Mrs Parry: 'Elwyn Roberts and the vicar of Llandegai will be on the top landing tonight, Mrs Parry. That is where your ghost is.'

I made a note to tell my bishop whom he could nobble for my job of exorcist after I retired.

We then settled down on the landing, Mr and Mrs Parry, Elwyn and I and the two girls, and we remained like Quakers at worship for about fifteen minutes, waiting for something to happen.

Elwyn and I had done a lot of this kind of waiting together over the years. Ours had been a peculiar sort of friendship – always meeting at night and invariably in someone else's house, with a couple of ghosts breathing down our necks, and other ghosts like children pretending to be shy, or performing all sorts of antics, in order to claim our attention. During quiet moments Elwyn and I would talk about all manner of things. I found him a knowledgeable person, but mostly we would talk about the paranormal, the peculiar things we had seen and that others claimed to have seen and reported in various papers, and we would exchange ideas and thoughts, as good friends should. I thought we had got to know each other pretty well. But how well is well? It was in the summer of 1975 that Elwyn shook me to the core. He made an appearance that left me absolutely speechless.

It was during the first week in August, the one week of the year when all good Welshmen make their pilgrimage to the Royal National Eisteddfod of Wales. The national Eisteddfod is held in North Wales and South Wales on alternate years. If, for any reason, good Welshmen are unable to attend the Eisteddfod, there are lesser obligations that they can and do perform. It is more or less an obligation to make for home and the TV set at 2 p.m. on the Tuesday of the first week in August and again at 2 p.m. on the Thursday of the first week in August. Tuesday at the Eisteddfod is the day of the crowning of the bard, and Thursday is the day when the bard of intricate metres is chaired. The names of both bards are kept a close secret. During the adjudication that precedes the crowning, the competitors are referred to by their pseudonyms. It is such an exciting time waiting to know. Will the chief bard this year be a North or a South Walian? He could be someone from near. He could even be someone from one's own town or village.

At the Cricieth Eisteddfod the adjudicator came to the end of his adjudication and called to the thousands in the pavilion and the pavilion field, 'My co-adjudicators and I are in total agreement that the very worthy winner of the crown for the year 1975 is the Gwion. Will the Gwion stand so that he may be escorted to the platform to be crowned?'

The trumpets are all at the ready. The little children with their garlands of flowers, dancing maidens with baskets of fruit, and bards of the druid circle are all ready to proceed from the platform to escort their new chief bard. This is the most exciting moment. The television cameras keep hovering over the heads of the vast audience. Then there is a crowd movement from the far side of the pavilion, a sort of ripple, and the cameras rush to focus themselves on a single lonely figure as he stands up to be escorted to the platform. Any minute now and the television commentator would recognize him and call out his name – but before anything was said, camera no. 1 got the new bard full frontal.

It was my Elwyn Roberts.

Apart from having said to me that he liked to read poetry as a boy, I had no idea that he was a serious poet. My Elwyn was being escorted to the stage to the sound of trumpets, and thousands of people in the audience were on their feet clapping and applauding their new chief bard.

He didn't look a bit like a chief bard sitting opposite me now on the bedroom landing waiting for a ghost. Then Elwyn broke the silence.

'She is coming,' he said, 'but very slowly. She is very shy and she is crying.'

This was my turn to talk to fresh air. I have never got over the embarrassment of doing this, the more so in this case when our two psychologist daughters were present.

'Come along and join us, my dear,' I said. 'We all want to help you.'

Then Elwyn's voice: 'She wants to tell us that she didn't kill her baby.'

And so it went on, she talking and Elwyn listening and interpreting for us.

I have on my files a copy of a letter that I wrote to the rector of the parish the day after our visit, dated 20 August 1983.

Dear Rector
You were quite right. The vibrations were far stronger on the landing than in either bedroom. We give you full marks.

The message we got was that the ghost was a single lady and a teacher named Margaret Ellis. We got a date 1836 and a figure 73. We also had a name Ernest Johnson, and a large white house concerned with mining of copper but not slate.

It appears that Margaret gave birth to an illegitimate child (John). Because she was a teacher the scandal was terrific. Ernest, the putative father, hired two vagabonds to kill the child. They threw the baby down the stairs or it fell in a struggle and died shortly after.

Local people refused to accept the tale about the vagabonds, and tongues wagged that Margaret Ellis had killed her baby. She left the district and went to Manchester, returning years later to die in the village.

We are quite happy that this is a good version of what happened, but it would be nice if we could check, and this could be done through your registers.

1836? Is it the date of Margaret's birth? Or date of tragedy? Possibly tragedy. Have you a baptism entry in your Church Register for Margaret Ellis 1800 and a funeral entry 1873? Have you any mention of an Ernest Johnson? This one actually should be on my register or St Gwynant's, Dwygyfylchi.

Where could she be teaching in 1836? Have you the names of teachers for the school? She could have taught at Pont Twr. She was musical and could also have been a freelance music teacher. If you can find anything out, I would be pleased.

Sincerely,
Aelwyn.

Reply from the rector:

Dear Aelwyn,
Thank you for your letter of 20th August regarding the ghost at ...

I have looked at the parish registers and have discovered that Margaret Ellis was buried at the Parish Church on March 27th, 1873. She was 76 years of age.

Following this I have looked at the Baptismal entries for the years 1797–1803, and the only entry of interest to us is one for a 'Margaret, the daughter of Owen and Catherine Ellis' dated May 30th, 1802. If this is the same Margaret who died in 1873 at the age of 76, then she was not baptised until she was 5 years. I gather that there was a large white house and also other habitations, and that there was a connection with copper mining.

I cannot find anything regarding Ernest Johnson, and I cannot find anything regarding the baptism or burial of an illegitimate child called John. It could well be that the tragedy took place during 1836 as you suggested, but the place of burial is unknown.

I called to see Mr & Mrs Parry the other day, and I was told that a reference was made to a church that did not have a tower or steeple. Could this be the old church, for the present church was not erected until 1842.

I was also invited upstairs to see whether or not I could feel any vibrations, and I am delighted to tell you that *no* vibrations were felt, and one felt that the atmosphere in the

house was warm and healthy, and one felt that Margaret Ellis is now at peace. Trusting that you are keeping well.
Sincerely
—

PS: I cannot find any reference to Margaret's teaching career at the school. If I do come across something I will let you know.

We had told Margaret that night that we believed her. We all did. Mr Parry said, 'I believe you, Margaret.' Mrs Parry said it. I said it. Elwyn said it, and the girls said it. Elwyn said she left the landing and the house with such a lovely smile on her face.

I think Margaret was the most 'human' of all the ghosts I have met. Bless her.

I think, too, that our two psychologist daughters were quite impressed. Margaret is probably the only ghost experience that either of them has had. I have never heard Bridget mention another.

Elwyn and I moved on to a very different one. Margaret had been so earnest and so humble. The one that followed her bordered on the schizophrenic.

17 The Extrovert Ghost

A very polite young man rang and asked if he could come and see me – to talk about a ghost problem. When he arrived, I began to wonder how sixth-formers became involved with ghosts, for he didn't look a day older than eighteen. He told me he was married, that he lived in an old converted farmhouse in Brynsiencyn, Anglesey, that he worked with a firm of insurance brokers in Bangor and that he was twenty-six years of age.

He told me that his name was Peter, his wife's name was Zoe and they had been married for just a year. They had been able to rent this old farmhouse on a year's lease at a very low rent. I forget how it had happened, unless it was a friend of theirs going overseas for a year on a sabbatical, and they were acting as tenant caretakers.

They had moved in in the November of the previous year and had been delightfully happy, meeting new friends and entertaining them in their 'olde worlde farm'.

'It was sometime last October that the trouble started,' said Peter. 'Zoe is a light sleeper, and she woke me up one night to tell me she thought there was a rat scratching underneath our bed.'

Peter listened for a long time and was just about to turn over to go to sleep again when the scratching restarted. He decided that, if this *was* a rat, it had to be a big one, and he remembered even at this time of crisis that he must put his shoes on – somehow he didn't fancy having bare feet while confronting a mammoth rat. He then tiptoed towards the window to retrieve his school cricket bat. While he was doing all this, the scratching seemed to work itself up to a steady crescendo. Zoe was so still and so quiet in the bed that he couldn't even hear her breathing.

'Zoe,' he whispered.

'Yes,' said a little voice.

'I've got the cricket bat. When I say "now", you pull the light cord above the bed and I'll slam with the bat. Now!'

The lights went on, the scratching stopped, the cricket bat crashed to the skirting-board. But there was no sign of a rat, dead or alive. They hunted around for quite a time, and then eventually Peter took off his shoes, placed the bat on the dressing-table and got back into bed. For the rest of the night they just lay there, unable to catch up with their sleep.

During his lunch hour next day Peter bought a couple of pounds of rat-poison. Liberal baits were set that night around the bedroom skirting-board. Peter even found one loose floor-board he could lift, and into this cavity he poured the contents of a whole packet. From time to time the baits were examined, and although none seemed to have been taken, there was no further scratching. Zoe thought the rat had gone away because it hated the smell of Peter's poison. But it hadn't. In mid-November they had another scratching session. This time Peter just hung over the side of the bed and shone his torch on the skirting-board. Nothing. So it went on, and Peter per-suaded Zoe that, even if it was a rat, it wasn't actually in the room. It was probably inside the skirting-board or in between the rafters or under the floorboards. Some nights there would be scratchings, and other nights it was quiet.

The big night was 20 December. Zoe had been wrapping up family Christmas presents, Peter was finishing off an estimate for a client, and they were late going to bed. The electric blanket had fused, the bed was freezing cold, and it took them ages to go to sleep. Peter said he thought it was three o'clock in the morning when he woke up. He realized that the bedclothes were being pulled away from him, and he was freezing cold, right down to the marrow of his bones. He opened his eyes, and not one foot away from his face was the incandescent face of a middle-aged woman leering at him. She stepped back from his bed and stood by the door, pointing an accusing finger at him. He tried to scream, but no sound came – and yet, somehow, something woke Zoe up. She gave a piercing scream, stood up in the bed, jumped right over Peter's inert body and ran down the stairs into the night. In some way Zoe's scream seemed to activate Peter, and he followed her down the stairs, out through the front door and along the little cart track to the next farm, where the young pyjamaed couple were given warmth, succour and time to recover from their state of shock.

I was able to check later that the couple had run barefoot, in their pyjamas, a distance of at least half a mile, and that night was particularly cold.

They made a pact that they would never, ever return to that awful house and meet that dreadful creature again. Peter broke the pact two days later when he returned to the house with his father to pick up their Christmas presents. It took ten minutes flat. He slammed the door after him, and the house had been empty ever since. They had spent Christmas and New Year with Peter's parents.

It was on 3 January that Peter rang to ask if he could come and see me. He told me on the phone that he had told his story to a gypsy lady and had asked her if she could explain what had happened to them. Apparently the gypsy had said: 'You must tell the priest of Llandegai.'

When he finished telling me his tale of woe, I knew there was no need for further checks. This young man was no hoaxer. A young couple would never have jumped out of their bed, half-naked, in the middle of the night, and run half a mile up a cart track to the nearest farm just for the fun of it. So there and then I rang Elwyn, and we arranged to visit the home the following Friday night.

It was arranged that Elwyn should pick me up at the vicarage at 7 p.m. and that we would pick up Peter (whose car was in dry-dock) at his office, and Zoe at the neighbouring farm. The four of us would go to the haunted farm together.

Peter started telling me, from the back seat, something he had forgotten to say when we met. Elwyn stopped him very quickly.

'Please don't say anything at all about what happened,' he said. 'It will only confuse things.'

We had to stop for petrol in Menai Bridge. Petrol was on ration at that time, but I can't for the life of me remember why. There was a queue of cars ahead of us, and while we crawled up slowly to the pump, Elwyn suddenly said:

'I think I know the name of the ghost that is troubling you. She is a short, middle-aged woman with straight grey bobbed hair. She has a tiny face and rustic cheeks, and she is dressed in a long brown dress made of some kind of blanket material – and she's got clogs on her feet.'

'That's right, that's right,' said Peter.

Then, a moment later, still in the petrol queue, Elwyn said: 'I think I have a name, too. The name that comes to me is "Hannah Roberts". But we'll find more when we get to your place.'

The house was cold when we opened the front door. No fire had been lit in it since before Christmas. Zoe put the kettle on the electric stove, and Peter proved himself to be an excellent fire-lighter. We drank our coffee and relaxed round the fire.

In no time at all Elwyn proclaimed: 'She's here all right! She is standing by the kitchen door, not sure whether to come further or not.' I could see nothing but, as always, took his word for it. 'Talk to her, Aelwyn,' said the medium.

'Come along, come nearer to us,' I said. 'We have come to your house to try to help you. You must tell us if there is something troubling you.'

It appears that at this our ghostly friend retreated from the room at the double, and Elwyn said: 'I think she is very shy.'

Elwyn is usually reliable and he doesn't often make glaring mistakes, but in this case he slipped up badly. Our ghost, Hannah Roberts, turned out to be anything but shy. She turned out to be a very extrovert ghost. Elwyn had hardly uttered the word 'shy' when she returned and this time, according to him, stood right by his chair ready to be questioned.

I explained to her that, in order to help her, we had to know something of the time when she lived. So could she tell us, perhaps, the name of the vicar of the parish? She very nearly spat the name out: 'Revd Parry – Revd Parry indeed. He was nothing,' she said, 'but a bloody snob. He didn't even see the ordinary people on the street but he'd scrape and bow to the gentry.'

She went on and on about the poor parson and then went off at a tangent to eulogize Lloyd George, the Prime Minister. It was 'Hip-hip-horray!' for Lloyd George, presumably because he was going to disestablish and disendow the Church in Wales and make a pauper of that old snob the Revd Parry.

The point was made and carefully demonstrated to us all that Hannah Roberts was not a member of the Anglican

Communion. So I timorously asked: 'What then is the name of your minister?'

'Minister?' said Hannah, 'Minister of God, he calls himself. That man is a minister of the Devil. Sending all our young men to the trenches to be killed.'

Elwyn and I knew immediately to whom she was referring. I have disguised most of the names of other villages and towns mentioned in this book, but the name of this village cannot be disguised. The village was Brynsiencyn, Anglesey. During the First World War years, 1914–18, Brynsiencyn had a pastor who was one of the great revivalist preachers of his day. The more pacifistic Nonconformists of the time were shaken to the core when this great preacher, John Williams of Brynsiencyn, accepted the King's Commission and became the recruiting officer whom Hannah described as the one who sent all the young men to the trenches to be killed.

Hannah was becoming quite exuberant, and I thought that any minute now she would forget and manifest herself. Having established her period of time, I began to question her as to why she had frightened the young people.

'They had done nothing to you,' I told her.

The answer came: 'Why don't they help me find the deeds of the farm then, the papers that William hid before he went to the war?'

Apparently the scratching noise had been Hannah trying to lift the loose board, or the skirting-board, to find the papers.

I was able to check on this afterwards. There had been no deeds because Hannah and William Roberts had been tenant farmers. But there must have been a tenancy agreement, and we did find that William, Hannah's husband, had been killed in the trenches.

There had been another young man killed in the trenches whose name was Ifan Hughes. Hannah was annoyed with me because I didn't know him. She told me his name was on the memorial plaque – a painted memorial, she said, and Ifan's name was sixth from the bottom. I thought it would be nice to see and photograph this plaque, and this memorial, so I pestered Hannah to tell me where I could find it. At first she said 'Bethesda', then she said Llangadwaladr, and after that she got angry, started to swear and became very evasive. Elwyn told me not to pursue this matter.

'Don't worry about it,' he said. 'I can see it. It is painted on a hoarding board outside a wooden memorial hall painted green, and it is true what she says: His name *is* sixth from the bottom.'

Later I hunted the length and breadth of Anglesey, but I failed to come across this little wooden village cenotaph with the name Ifan Hughes carved sixth from the bottom.

Hannah just talked and talked. It was as if she was glad to have someone to listen to her. She mentioned the names of several men, but time and again she came back to Ifan Hughes. We came to the conclusion that both William Roberts, her husband, and this Ifan Hughes, who could have been her brother, had been killed. Hannah became silly, giggly, and refused to speak any more of Ifan Hughes. Then Elwyn told us she had left us.

The tension was broken. Zoe went to make tea, Peter put more coal on the fire. Elwyn and I compared notes, as we invariably did.

We were still drinking tea when Elwyn said: 'She's coming back.'

I heard a little intake of breath from Peter and Zoe. They were both sitting bolt upright on the settee. Zoe's mouth was wide open, and she was pointing towards the kitchen door.

'Can you see anything?' I said to them.

'There! There!' said Zoe, still pointing.

I looked and there was the faint outline of a woman. As I peered, it became plainer. She was a little woman in her sixties, with the kind of short grey hair that Elwyn had described, and she had the red cheeks of an outdoor person. Her face was red and weather-beaten. She was a nice, homely old lady. This was Hannah, the extrovert, who couldn't resist the chance to shock us and to take centre stage. Hannah was enjoying herself. Then, just as suddenly as she had come, she disappeared again.

Elwyn talked to the young couple. He explained that, for them to have had this ghostly experience, one or both was probably a focus person (afterwards we agreed it was Zoe), and it was because of this that Hannah was able to show herself. We explained that there was no danger, that Hannah just wanted to share her old house with them.

The youngsters said they were no longer afraid.

'Now that we have seen Hannah properly,' they said, 'we don't mind at all.'

The next day I rang the vicar of the parish and told him a little of our experiences of the previous evening. I asked if there would be anyone in the parish who had lived there during the First World War.

'Yes,' he said, 'there is my churchwarden and his wife. Both are in their eighties, but their memories are perfectly sound.'

I met the old folk the following day.

'Can you remember who farmed Gelli Fair before the war?' I asked.

'William and Hannah Roberts,' they said without the slightest hesitation.

'What happened to them?'

'William was killed at the Battle of Ypres,' said the warden.

'And Hannah?' I asked.

'Hannah stayed on for a bit, and then there was trouble about the tenancy agreement. Hannah didn't think it right for her to be moved from the farm when her husband had given his life for his country. The squire offered her a cottage on the estate. She refused. Then she married a man from Conwy, but after his death she came back to live in the village.'

'What do you know about Ifan Hughes?' I asked.

The old couple knew nothing of him, but the old man did say: 'Hannah was a very attractive young widow, and I believe she had a good number of offers of marriage before she married her second husband. Ifan Hughes could have been one of the suitors.'

'I take it,' I said, 'that she was not a church member.'

The old chap threw up his arms. 'Hannah Roberts hated the Episcopal Church and all it stood for,' he said. 'She was Nonconformist to the core, and she used to abuse the poor vicar in public, called him the squire's puppet. I remember one night after a Church Disestablishment meeting in the big chapel, a stone was thrown through our window, and my wife and I are convinced, to this day, that it was Hannah, Gelli Fair, who threw that stone.'

'Was she a regular chapel-goer?' I asked.

'As regular as a clock,' said the old man. 'Three times every Sunday, wet or fine, you would see Hannah making her way to chapel, and always early.'

Then the warden's wife chipped in: 'Yes, but you remember, Alun, during the war years she left Capel Mawr, and she used to walk every Sunday to the next village, Llangadwaladr.'

'I'd forgotten that,' said the old man. And then, with a chuckle, he added, 'And the Sunday the Revd John Williams left the pastorate, Hannah was back in her old seat in her old chapel as if nothing had happened.'

That afternoon I visited the village cemetery and stood by the grave of Hannah Roberts, who had been buried in 1962, aged eighty-seven. It was a strange feeling standing by the overgrown grave of the lady I had been talking to the previous evening.

Some days after the event, I rang Peter and Zoe to see if they were back and to enquire if they were all right. They were fine apparently.

'But,' said Peter, 'Hannah is still with us. She hasn't gone away.'

'I'm sorry you are still being troubled,' I told him. 'I will contact Elwyn and see what else can be done.'

Then came the pleading voice of Peter: 'Oh no, please don't bother. We don't want to get rid of her any more. Now that we have seen her, and she's such a lovely old lady, we don't mind.'

So we left things as they were.

Months later someone asked me if I had heard of a young couple living in a haunted house in Anglesey. Apparently they would invite friends to a ghost party (Bring your own eats and drinks.) and regale their friends with the story of Hannah and how she used to live in this house, and how one night they actually saw her. Some of the guests would say they didn't believe in ghosts. There would follow a conducted tour of the house, and every cupboard was opened to show the visitors there was no one hiding in the bedrooms. Then all would sit quietly in the living-room, and Peter would put on a strange voice and call out:

'Hannah, we have some present who do not believe. Prove to them, Hannah, that you are still living here in your old house. At the count of three you will knock twice!'

Peter would then, in his best entrepreneur voice, count to three, and Hannah would give two resounding knocks on the bedroom floor. Party-goers' spines would tingle.

After hearing of the parties, I couldn't help thinking that, of all those present at the Old Farmhouse, the one who would enjoy the party most would be Hannah the Ghost.

PART TWO

Mediums and Their Gifts

1   *The Gifts*

Mediumism is most certainly a gift. I am not sure whether it is a gift to be coveted. My medium friends tell me that the clamour of spirits, from the other side, to use their minds and bodies, can at times be very tiring, and often they have to be quite firm and tell persistent ghosts to go away, to get lost or find someone else for a change.

It is, I think, a sort of gift that carries with it a great deal of responsibility. I have often come away from a house leaving a spirit still earthbound, or what I thought was an earthbound spirit, in order to get to the late chip shop before it closed. There was nothing I could do for the poor spirit, even if I forfeited my chips, but I'm sure it must be difficult for a medium not to complete a job.

I find that it is a gift that brings little reward. Most mediums are, however, compensated by having other gifts. Most of them are able to heal, a very great number enjoy the gift of clairvoyance and psychometry, a good number are able to divine water and enjoy all the other fun things, such as pendulum-swinging and map-dowsing, that go along with water-divining.

Ask them about any of these gifts and they will put on a humble act that annoys me so much.

'Oh!' they say. 'Why do you ask? Anyone can heal if they try' or 'We all have the gift of clairvoyance' or, 'God has given to all the gift of water-divining.'

2   *Telepathy*

My medium friends, for all their gifts and versatility, don't seem to have knowledge of the gift of telepathy. I wish I had this gift, if only to get my own back on them and say, 'Telepathy? It is quite easy really. Everyone has the gift of telepathy.' I have never known a single one who lays claim to this gift of mind-to-mind communication.

We are told that, over the past two decades, the Soviets have spent vast fortunes trying to cultivate this gift. They see telepathy as the most practical way of making contact with other, possibly intelligent, beings on other planets in the universe.

The last time I heard exciting tales of telepathy was when, as a fascinated young curate, I sat at the feet of the then 80-year-old Captain Williams of Nantlle. Old Captain Williams had been trading as captain of his own sailing ship. As a regular trader he had become well known along the coast of West Africa. This part of Africa today is fast becoming a tourist haven, but in Captain Williams' day it was described as 'the White Man's Grave'.

Captain Williams would describe how, having been chartered to take a cargo of merchandise to some West African port, he had then to use his own initiative to find a profitable cargo for the return journey. After discharging the London cargo, it was his custom to leave the ship with a skeleton crew and proceed with the rest of the crew into the interior to scrounge for cargo. Apparently he and his men were welcomed by most of the tribes they visited.

It took many days to complete a business deal. The greetings, the exchange of presents, and the countless little feastings and revelries that African PR required at that time took many days. The crew would have set up their tents on the outskirts of the village, and the captain a short distance aft.

The old captain, always a light sleeper, described how, every morning, shortly after daybreak, Manga Wanga, the witch doctor, would walk into the village, always from the same direction, and how all the villagers seemed to know the hour of his coming and would gather in one place to hear him. Manga Wanga would mount a small pulpit, and his congregation would all stand quietly, eagerly awaiting his message. The witch doctor would then regale the villagers with lurid stories of happenings in other tribes.

Did they remember that great warrier, Malu, of the Isu tribe who had so often fought against them? The congregation would shout, 'Yes! Yes! We do. Malu the great. We all remember Malu.' There would then be a pause, and the witch doctor would dramatically tell them that Malu would fight no more. He had been caught in the act of stealing from his chief's brother and had had his right hand cut off. There followed a great crowd reaction of ooing and tutting. Then came news of the Icawawe tribe: the chief's son was to be married to the girl Achia. And so on and on – not just a recitation of the news from different tribes but live drama. When it came to the news item that Chief Lukuwaio of the Maleki tribe had had a recurrence of his lumbago attacks, Manga Wanga walked around the camp bent double and groaned so loudly that the dogs barked.

This happened in the life of the camp every single morning. The witch doctor not only brought the news of the known world to his tribe but enacted it for them. It was almost TV and not radio.

So the old captain kept awake one moonlit night, and when, an hour before dawn, he saw the witch doctor slinking out of the village, he followed him. Captain Williams said, 'I was not a great tracker, and looking back along the years I'm sure that Manga Wanga knew very well that I was following.'

He came to a small clearing and at the far end there was a small, treeless hill and a well-trodden path leading to its summit. As Manga took the path, the sea captain kept out of sight. He told me that the witch doctor stood on that hill for nearly an hour, and as he stood, he quietly swayed backwards and forwards. He was receiving messages, news items, from the witch doctors of neighbouring tribes. Some of them were more than fifty miles away as the crow flies. At one point, after about ten minutes, Manga raised both hands above his head and stood on tiptoe. This was the time, the captain thought, when it was Manga's turn to relay his tribal news items to the others.

Captain Williams was convinced that he had witnessed a most sophisticated telepathic communication system.

I asked him if he thought there could be a limit to the distance over which such messages could be relayed. He didn't think distance had anything to do with it, and then he told me a tale about a farm in South Africa.

On this farm the white farmer and the native workforce normally got on well together. One day the farmer came out to the compound because the natives were wailing and making the most dismal noises. He found them cowering together, obviously terrified of someone or something. He called the head boy, who would normally greet him quite casually, but this time he crawled up to him on his tummy and proceeded to lick his boots.

'What is it, Laraka?' he asked, and Laraka replied, 'Oh, White Master! Six evil black men have killed a white man far away, and now we know that all white men will be angry, and black people will be punished.'

This incident happened apparently at the turn of the century, when the morse code telegraph system in Africa was very primitive, being tapped out cross-country from one station to another. It was four days before the official news came to the farm that a white man had been lynched by six natives in the Sudan.

We circle the earth, and we can walk on the moon, but Captain Williams told me over forty years ago that there lived in Africa at that time men who could relay and receive a message over a distance of thousands of miles by merely tuning their minds to the correct wavelength.

3 Clairvoyance

Some people call clairvoyance 'second sight'. I prefer Winnie Marshall's description. She compares a medium who has this gift to a car-driver who keeps his eyes diligently on the road ahead and yet is able to see in his mirror all the things going on behind him. Winnie tells me that regularly she can see these pictures, or images, floating before her eyes. She has no idea what most of the pictures are – they're just like the traffic and people that come behind us on the motorway. Sometimes the car-driver will announce, 'There's a police car coming up behind us' or, 'There's a new registration Rover just going to overtake.'

Winnie tells me that very often the same thing happens to the mirror images of the clairvoyant.

Her favourite story is the one about her first grandson. In the flotsam of images going past one day she saw a picture of a little baby boy, and she thought, 'That could be one of ours with that likeness,' so she called him back to have a closer look. She decided that this baby certainly had the Marshall look, and so she decided to wait.

Two weeks later her daughter came to visit her.

'Mum,' she said, 'I went to the doctor last night, and he says I'm two months pregnant. You're going to be a gran.'

Winnie got her knitting-needles together and went out to buy stacks of blue wool.

That, very simply, I think, is what clairvoyance is all about. The pictures revolve, and the trained, experienced clairvoyant is able to fit them together in some semblance of a pattern.

Psychometry is just a special form of clairvoyance. If you are physically present with the clairvoyant – and particularly if you allow the clairvoyant to hold something that belongs to you, a wallet or a watch or car keys – pictures cease to be a sort of general index of unrelated scenes, objects and people: they become pictures that relate to you alone. And here again the art or the cleverness is not so much in the seeing of visions but in placing them together and interpreting them.

I have always been terrified of having my fortune told, even in fun by Mrs Ponsonby-Brown, dressed as a gypsy, at the church bazaar. When I decided to write about my medium friends and their gifts, I was determined to use only first-hand information and write only about the things that I myself had seen and experienced, so that like St John at the end of the fourth gospel I might be able to say: 'This is the disciple that beareth witness of these things and wrote these things: and we know that his witness is true.'

Winnie Marshall can tell wonderful tales of things that have happened to her, in her own life and in the lives of friends and clients as a result of her clairvoyant visions. But I knew that I would have to put temptation behind me and conquer my great fear of having my fortune told if I was to bear true testimony. It was with fear and trembling that I did, one day, ask Winnie for a psychometry demonstration. I knew I could trust her ... I dutifully handed over my wallet to her. She took it, held it tightly to her breast and started to sway a little, but she was smiling and I took comfort from the fact that she was smiling. I am not going to say what Winnie Marshall said to me – that is our secret. But she did tell me sufficient about my past and about my aspirations for the future for me to know that she, and many others like her who are grouped together as fortune-tellers, have a very real gift, and they certainly have some peculiar pre-knowledge of things to come. Having said this I can almost hear my scientist friend and colleague Elwyn protesting at my logic (or lack of it) so I will rephrase and draw from my experience a more logical conclusion and say that Winnie Marshall, in my opinion, seems to have an abundance of the gifts of clairvoyancy and psychometry.

One evening I watched a psychomotry competition between heavyweights. My churchwarden, the Lady Janet Douglas Pennant, had a very good friend, Lady Laura McConnell, a retired Harley Street consultant who was an excellent medium. When she was coming to stay at Penrhyn for a few days, Lady Janet thought it would be nice if Lady Laura and Elwyn could meet, so Elwyn and I were invited to Penrhyn for the evening. After a very nice meal we all retired to the sitting-room, and it started. Lady Laura just leaned over towards Elwyn and held out her hand.

'Your watch,' she said, and off it came. Then Lady Laura started to regale Elwyn with his life's problems and a forecast of how they would be resolved. At this stage I had come to know Elwyn well, and he had confided to me a great deal about his family and his work, and about his hopes and aspirations. As Lady Laura built up the pictures together, I just gaped in amazement. I remember thinking to myself, 'I hope Elwyn won't think that I have told Lady Laura all these things about him.'

She was so very, very accurate, and Elwyn was giving nothing away. Statement after statement was so true that I wanted to call out to her, 'You are so right. That did happen to Elwyn.' But Elwyn said nothing. He just sat there with his eyes closed and not saying a word. Presumably this is how you do act in a psychometry competition.

I well remember Lady Laura's saying, 'I see a door. This door is your office or your laboratory door, and you are trying to open it. It is an experiment, and it's not showing the expected results. You feel depressed about it, and you are wondering if this door is ever going to open for you. Don't give up. The door will open.'

Elwyn had told me about this experiment that seemed to be going on and on and on. Now Lady Laura was saying that he would succeed with it. Elwyn just said a polite 'Thank you' at the end of it all. Lady Laura returned his watch and gave him her own.

Elwyn closed his eyes, and then he began: 'I see you with a rope around you, and there are other young women roped together. You are climbing a mountain, and you are the leader.'

'Good for you,' said Lady Laura. 'You're going back some time.' She told us the name of the first mountain to be climbed by an all-female team.

'And I see a small single plane,' said Elwyn, 'and the markings on the fuselage are CSC 24.'

Lady Laura gave a loud guffaw. 'Bless my soul, that was

the first plane I ever had. Fancy that one turning up.'

We all had a wonderful evening. None of those present would ever say that he disbelieved in psychometry.

I shall never, to my dying day, forget the psychometry that Winnie practised on me the first evening we met. It was the night on which we visited the scene of the council house ghost. I didn't understand it at all at that time. Winnie was finding it very difficult to enter into a trance after just meeting me, a perfect stranger. My images were strong and were flooding in on her. She would go half way into a trance and have to come back again.

'Sorry,' she said, 'I just can't concentrate. Please can you tell me why I see you with pound notes sticking to your fingers?'

This amazed me. Whilst I was waiting for her and Elwyn to pick me up at the vicarage, I realized that I had a crumpled bundle of pound notes in my hip pocket. I decided, as I wouldn't need money that night, to leave them at home. I was smoothing them out and putting them away in my desk when the door-bell rang and they arrived. I told Winnie all this, and she tried to go off a second time but failed, and this time she asked me, 'Can you make any sense of this? You are entering a house, and you are being welcomed by a happy-looking lady in a floral dress covered in a vast white apron. This lady is walking into a fire, or a big furnace, and as she enters it she is turning round to you, and she is smiling at you and beckoning you to follow her, and you do follow into the furnace; minutes later she walks out of the fire unscathed, and she closes the furnace door with you still inside.

This one took just a little longer, and then I got it. The house was in my parish. The lady was Emily, a very timid and a very innocent spinster lady who was a faithful parishioner of mine and who had died a year ago. She lived in an old farmhouse, and it had such a large seated inglenook that it had a curtain across to divide it from the rest of the room. Six people, three aside, could actually sit inside that inglenook fireplace. On cold winter afternoons I would very often end my pastoral visits at Emily's. There would be such a welcome! She would escort me to the inglenook with its heaped-up coal fire, then she would leave me and draw the curtain, to keep away the draught, whilst she went off to the kitchen to brew the tea and butter the newly baked Welsh cakes. Only Emily and I, of all the people in the world, knew of these little treats, but somehow there was a picture of it, and Winnie had focused on it.

And then she reminded me of something sad.

'I see now a young boy sitting on the edge of a boat or a raft. The boat is in the middle of a deep, dark lake. The boy becomes stiff and he falls off the side of the boat into the water. I wait for him to surface but there is nothing. The lake is perfectly still, and there is not a ripple, and there is no sign of the boy in the dark waters.'

Three years before, on a Sunday afternoon in the summer, I had heard the sirens of the fire service going past the house. Someone telephoned me to say that John had fallen into the lake and had been drowned and that his mother was away and expected back at eight o'clock that evening. If no one else would, I knew it would have to be me that gave her the awful news.

I was sitting there with her after she had come back and she had been telling me how John hated water. He had water phobia – he would never go into the sea or stand on the bank of a lake or a river. And she was now being told that John had been drowned in that dark lake near their house and that he had gone to it of his own volition. Three students came into the room – they were the lads who were in lodgings next door.

'We are so sorry,' they said. 'We were with John when it happened. We had made a raft and we were going to test it. John came with us. He did say he was afraid of water but he wanted to conquer his fear, and as he knew the three of us could swim, he would risk it. We sat on that raft, two on the left and two on the right, and pushed it to the centre of the lake. We sat like that for a bit, and then John became very stiff. He seemed drawn into the water. He just doubled up and fell in. We waited for him to come up but he never did. We dived and dived into the very depths but could find no trace of him. Then Peter ran to call the Fire Brigade.'

'But please believe us,' said the leader. 'We did try so very hard. He fell in and never came up again, and there was not a ripple on the face of the water.'

And here was Winnie, seeing the thing over again and

saying exactly the same thing: 'There was not a ripple on the face of the water.'

Not in a thousand years will I understand these strange gifts that belong to these very gifted friends of mine.

4   *Healing*

During the earthly life of Jesus, it was invariably the Master himself who laid hands on the sick and the maimed and the blind. The disciples followed him and watched how it was done.

On one occasion, when Jesus had taken Peter, John and James with him to the Mount of the Transfiguration, a father brought his son who was possessed of a devil to be cured. The remaining disciples laid their hands on the young lad; they did everything they had seen Jesus do, and yet the boy's spasms became heavier and heavier until it became clear that he was at the point of death. Crowds had gathered round and were deriding the disciples, and the poor father, who had brought his child to the disciples, was beside himself with grief. Then Jesus arrived, assessed the situation and turned to tell his disciples of the illness they were dealing with, and its cure. It was apparently a kind of devil-possession that could be combated only by faith, prayer and fasting.

During the life of Jesus the disciples seemed so clumsy and ineffective. Then something terrific happened to them on the first Pentecost, and the lovely, lovely stories in the Acts of the Apostles illustrate so well the courage and the endurance and the spiritual powers that the post-Pentecost disciples now possessed.

The story I like best is the one describing Peter's cure of the lame man – lame, we are told, 'from his mother's womb'. Every day his family or kind friends would carry him to the gate of the Temple called Beautiful, so that he could, as a cripple, beg for alms. When he saw Peter and John approaching his little patch, he rattled his box and called, 'Alms, alms' to them. The disciples stopped, and Peter, we are told, 'fastened his eyes upon him' and said to him, 'Silver and gold have I none, but what I have, that I give thee. In the name of Jesus Christ of Nazareth, walk.' The courage of it! No preliminaries, no preconditions such as faith and repentance. He didn't even touch the patient. He just looked at him and said, 'In the name of Jesus Christ of Nazareth, walk,' and the man walked.

There are, throughout the world today, many, many ministers of religion and lay members of the Christian Churches who are healing in the name of Jesus Christ of Nazareth. They have the faith that, as they lay their hands on the sick, Jesus of Nazareth will lay his hands over their hands and enable them to bring about the cure that can be done only by 'prayer and fasting'. These people believe that the wonderful cures they bring about are wrought by Christ himself, with them acting as his earthly hands and feet.

The power is not of the Church. The healing power is within certain individual members of the Church. It is not a gift that the Church can pass on in its sacraments. The priest at his ordination is given authority to forgive sins, but no special healing powers are given at ordination. Now the Church seems anxious to recapture this great talent that the early Church so treasured, and to encase it, once again, as part of its new liturgy.

In the Spiritualist Church it is different. Healing is an integral part of its worship. Members would expect their minister to have healing powers. It could be that a lay member had the gift in greater abundance, but they would still expect the minister to be able to lay healing hands on the sick. Mediumship and healing, in the Spiritualist Church, seem to go hand in hand. It has, however, to be remembered that not all mediums are Spiritualists.

Winnie Marshall is a Spiritualist. She was brought up in the Spiritualist Church and showed special gifts and talents even as a child. She has given demonstrations in several countries in Europe and is in constant demand as a medium throughout Britain. This year she has been made a full minister of her church.

Elwyn Roberts, on the other hand, is not a Spiritualist. I suspect that he is a good old-fashioned Welsh Methodist. He invites me to say a prayer before we begin our sessions and a priestly blessing – on the house and its occupants, both earthly and spiritual – before we leave.

Winnie and Elwyn are the products of very different religious backgrounds. It is not surprising to find that their ideas about spiritual gifts differ greatly. Elwyn would agree with others that healing is a gift given by nature or God to all mankind. He would probably say, too, that it is a gift which God gives to all mankind. If the gift is discovered and treasured, it will become stronger with use, and others will derive more benefit from it. If the gift is allowed to remain dormant, it will, over the years, rust away and become useless.

Winnie Marshall would agree with Elwyn that the gift, like all good things, comes from God. But for Winnie the gift is received not directly but through the guide spirits. I have no idea which interpretation is the true one, but I can vouch for the healing powers of both the healers. If, as Elwyn says, God gave him the power, I can testify that Elwyn for his part has kept it shiny and sharp.

I remember being out on a ghost job with Elwyn many years ago on a cold, damp November evening. We were working, on this particular night, in an unfurnished house, from which, two years before, the tenants had fled because of ghost hauntings. The landlord had now decided to revive his property investment with a little refurnishing and refurbishing and a spot of de-ghosting, before reletting to other tenants. When we got to the house, it was quite derelict. No electricity, no heating and nearly all the windows smashed. Elwyn and I found two boxes to sit on and put our calor-gas lantern on the floor between us. I was feeling cold and depressed and sorry that I had ever consented to come, and one of my knees was swollen and aching.

My knee had been troublesome for quite a long time. It had swollen to twice its normal size and had become extremely painful – a dull, always-there, never-goes-away sort of pain. I had been to the doctor, and he had prescribed anti-inflammatory capsules and arranged for me to have out-patient physiotherapy at our local hospital. But after weeks of therapy the knee remained painful and stubbornly swollen.

This night the particular ghost we wished to contact was playing hard to get, so I thought that, taking everything into consideration, this might be a good time to seek a spot of healing. I told Elwyn about my knee and that the doctor had said that it was probably a mixture of arthritis and old age. Elwyn asked which knee and got hold of it firmly with his two hands. In that cold room, in which the rest of me was nearly dying of hypothermia, I could feel my knee becoming warmer and warmer, hotter and hotter, under Elwyn's hands. After about three minutes he released my knee. The pain had gone, and within about a fortnight the swelling had also gone. If anyone asked me today which one was my swollen, arthritic knee of years ago, I wouldn't know. Elwyn had somehow or other radiated into my unhealthy knee some of the health-giving rays, or currents, or vibrations, from within his own body.

Some years after my knee cure I met a friend who on Sunday was a church organist, and a pianist for the Liverpool Philharmonic Orchestra during the week. We enquired after each other's health, and he told me that he was fine again, thanks to my friend Elwyn. He went on to say that about six months earlier he had been in agony with a tennis elbow. He had tried everything, and the doctor had tried everything, but nothing would persuade the tennis to leave the elbow. Playing the organ was torture, but playing the piano for hours on end with the orchestra was just plain hell. One Saturday morning he had bumped into my friend Elwyn Roberts on Mostyn High Street, Llandudno, apparently 'just about where we are standing at the present moment', he said. Elwyn had asked him how he was, just as I had, and he had told Elwyn he was fine except for his tennis elbow. Elwyn had asked him which elbow, and there on Mostyn Street he had got hold of his elbow and squeezed it hard for two or three minutes – and he had been all right ever since.

Years later I had to beg treatment for another ailment from Winnie Marshall. Now Winnie would have me know that when she heals she is always assisted by two or more spirit guides. The guides diagnose for her, and they report to her on the amount of dosage radiation to give.

Probably the best-known Spiritualist healer was the late Harry Edwards. In the 1950s he became a household name. He not only healed the sick who were brought to his clinics but was also able to perform 'absent healing'. Towards the end of his life he reduced the scale of his clinic healings so that he could reach out to many more sick people through his absent healing programme.

I remember, many years ago, visiting a very good and very devout member of my congregation. She told me how the milkman had told her about his 5-year-old daughter. The little girl had never walked. She had been a patient at different hospitals for months on end. She was now attending the local hospital as an out-patient. Doctors offered very little hope that she would ever walk. My parishioner had asked the milkman to write on a piece of paper for her the medical name of the child's illness, and she had it in front of her. She told me that she had dropped a line to Harry Edwards about her – just as if dropping a line to Harry Edwards about any sick person was the most natural thing in the world to do.

Later on, I found that it very nearly *was* the most natural thing to do, particularly amongst a rapidly growing group of people who admired him. I am quite sure that Britain's Roman Catholic and Anglican bishops would have been shocked at that time, the mid 1950s, if they had known how many of the faithful of their flocks were sending letters to Harry Edwards, the Spiritualist, asking for his prayers and for absent healing. I know of a good number of people who wrote and were made better, and our milkman's daughter is now a very healthy mother of three lovely children.

Harry Edwards always maintained that he had the assistance of Pasteur and Lister, and that he was able to carry out absent healing because his guide spirits travelled great distances for him, quite unfettered. He himself spent many, many hours on his knees every day.

At that time I knew a wonderful priest healer of the Anglican Church. He had his clinic in Harley Street and was always the last referral point for the Harley Street sick. He said to me once, 'Old Harry is a wonderful healer, but I do wish he would get rid of this foolish notion of his that he is being guided by Lister and Pasteur.'

Winnie Marshall has the same spiritual belief as Harry Edwards. She heals with the assistance of her spirit guides. I found that a desperate man never argues with the label on the bottle if the effect is good.

Last year I planned a May walking holiday in Greece. Ten

weeks exactly from the day I was to start my holiday, I got out of bed and put my weight on my right foot on the bedroom floor, and a searing pain shot up my leg. It was just as if I had stepped on a two-inch nail, and for the rest of the morning it was painful, but the pain wore off during the day. It was definitely not the kind of heel for a hiking holiday in hot Greece. Next day it was the same, hobbling in pain all morning but better in the evening. I wasted valuable time trying out different medications that Boots' Chemist had to offer.

When I saw my GP, we agreed that, as the holiday date was looming nearer, we needed a specialist quick. He very kindly referred me to an orthopaedic surgeon. For the specialist apparently, it was an easy diagnosis. The fact that pain was worse in the morning and tended to disappear during the day was a good clue, and the shootingness of the pain was another. He told me, 'You have a trapped nerve in your heel' and, as if to endorse his diagnosis, he pressed his thumb deep into a certain spot on my heel. 'The seat of the pain is there,' he said. I very nearly touched the ceiling. I told him about my planned holiday in Greece and that if I had to cancel it I didn't think I would be able to arrange another.

'No problem,' said the specialist. He could cure my heel almost overnight by giving me a cortisone injection. On the other hand, I had six weeks to go, and he suggested a gentler cure at the hands of the physiotherapists. I attended their clinics twice a week, and they connected me to a deep heat machine.

One week from D-Day, when I reported back to my consultant, I was still no better. He called for the nurse to hold my leg, got out a syringe that seemed as thick as a six-inch nail, filled it with cortisone and jabbed it right on target. He cheerfully told me that my heel would be painful for the whole of the next day, not because of the trapped nerve but because of the damage his syringe would have done getting through to it. 'The day after tomorrow,' he said, 'your pain will have disappeared completely.'

But the day after tomorrow was three days before I was due to go to Greece, and the pain, when I got out of bed, was as bad as it ever had been. So there was nothing for it but to hobble into the car and make my way to Winnie Marshall's house in Colwyn Bay.

I told Winnie about my pain and about my holiday predicament. She wasn't particularly interested in the surgeon's diagnosis. Sandal off, and Winnie bade me sit on the settee and held my foot in her hands.

'Relax, for goodness sake,' said Winnie. 'I'm not going to hurt you.'

'I *am* relaxed,' I told her, and Winnie's reply to that was, 'You may be relaxed but your foot isn't.'

At this, she began to massage my foot, then she slapped it and twisted it for a good ten minutes before she let it go. I felt an immediate improvement – the pain was gone, I thought, and I told her so. Winnie was so disappointed.

'All that was just to get you to relax your foot,' she said. 'I haven't given you any healing yet.'

But she had touched my foot. I had been five weeks with the physiotherapists, and none of them had laid a finger of my foot. They had connected me up to a machine that was supposed to radiate deep warmth. I felt no warmth, and there was no little bulb or anything on it to give any indication that it was even plugged into the mains. There were notices everywhere that if the machine even became warm against your flesh you were to ring a bell. I never had occasion to ring the bell, nor, during the whole time I was there, did I hear anyone else's bell of distress ringing. But Winnie had taken my heel into her warm hands; she had rubbed it and massaged it and slapped it, and cared for it, and I felt that after one session the pain had gone. But Winnie's healing had not begun yet.

I sat on the settee beside her. She held my foot against her body and started to sway and at the same time hum a little tune. I could feel the warmth of her hand on my heel – the same kind of warmth that Elwyn, years before, had somehow injected into my knee. After about four minutes Winnie slapped my foot and let it go.

'There you are,' she said. 'My guides tell me that your heel is now cured and that there will be no need for you to come back.'

Days later I flew to Greece, and with haversack on my back I walked miles without feeling the slightest twinge of pain. The same heel has taken me up and down the Carneddi and the Glyder mountains dozens of times since then.

*

It is people who have never seen a ghost who say they don't believe in ghosts. It is people who have never received the benefit of spiritual healing who call it quackery. I went to two healers asking them to make me better, to take away my pain. They were polite and patient with me. Others could have said to me, 'We are not here to make people better and to heal odd parts of their bodies. We work to make a person whole again.' I don't quite know what the difference is – or at least I didn't before I sent a friend of mine suffering from a terminal illness to their healing circle.

Tom had lived under the threat of death for over three months. The doctors had told him that there was no cure, and he didn't expect a cure, but he attended every single healing service in the local Spiritualist church. He gained so much from knowing these kind, healing people. He died without panic or kerfuffle. I suppose the healers would say he died a 'whole man'.

It was the same with my parishioner who died of cancer at the age of forty-seven. Her husband told me after her death, 'She wouldn't have missed a single healing session of theirs for all the world, and she died so serenely.'

These healing people say that we all have the gift of healing, that we could all stand at the gate of the Temple called Beautiful and say, 'Silver and gold have I none, but what I have, that I give thee. In the name of Jesus Christ of Nazareth, walk.'

How I wish I had the courage.

5 Water-Divining – Dowsing

Eureka! Eureka! I am not absolutely thick, nor am I entirely giftless. I can divine water. I can dowse. I am a radiesthian. All this happened to me a few days before I was due to submit my manuscript to the publishers. One event led to another, kind friends introduced me to other kind friends, so day by day I was making new and exciting discoveries.

It started off when I made tentative enquiries amongst medium friends for knowledge of someone who could divine water. Not one of them knew a water-diviner. I then asked round my non-Spiritualist friends, and Farmer Ken Ellis remembered that years ago he had had a wonderful shepherd working for him who divined water. He told me how, whenever the fields got clogged up with water and to prevent his sheep becoming lame with foot-rot, Richard Owen, the shepherd, would cut hazel twigs from the hedges and trace and mark all the twenty-six drain lengths running through the farm. He would find the ones that were clogged to enable the men to dig straight down to the cloggage without scarring the fields with trial-and-error digs.

The problem was that Richard Owen had been retired many years and was now in his eighty-fourth year, but we found him. He had retired to Gaerwen in Anglesey and was thrilled to be able to do little odd jobs on a farm near his home. I went to see him one evening and told him that I was writing a book about the paranormal and asked if he would give me a demonstration of water-divining. No problem, apparently. If I could provide the hazel sticks and meet him the following afternoon at the farm where he worked, he would show me how it was done.

The following morning I found the hazel trees in Penrhyn Park and cut a good supply of sticks to Richard Owen's specification. The twigs had to be Y-shaped, the leg of the Y just two inches or so to allow it to revolve, and the V part about twelve inches in length. The diameter, not all that important, anything from a quarter to three-quarters of an inch.

Richard Owen was waiting for me on the farmyard and was rather amused by the vast selection of hazel branches I had brought with me. He chose one of the thinner, quarter-inch-diameter twigs, for his first demonstration. He took the twig and me to a place where he knew there was water. He held the V stalks of the twig in his upturned palms – held them very tightly – and he tucked his elbows into his rib cage. No sooner did he stand on the spot where there was water than the Y leg of the twig started rotating in an anticlockwise direction, the tail gyrating over and over, Richard holding tight to the two V sides. The inevitable had to happen: the twig began to tear at its joint and within seconds had splintered and broken itself in half.

Before the first twig had fallen to the ground, the enthusiastic learner had pulled out another from the boot of his car. I stood with it over the exact spot on which Richard had stood. I held it tightly in my upturned palms, just as Richard had; I even said a little prayer – which I don't think Richard had. Absolutely nothing happened. There was not a quiver from the stick. I was bitterly disappointed.

Richard Owen suggested that we go the field opposite. He knew that this particular field had umpteen hidden streams. For his next trick he helped himself to the thickest of my branches, one with a one-inch diameter. We walked across the field, Richard leading, me following, Richard holding on tightly to the stick. All of a sudden I saw him being pulled forward and his elbows jutting out at the back. With the instinct of those who enjoy gawping at accidents, I took two steps forward so that I could see him better. He was using all his strength to prevent the stick from twisting and burning his hands. The demand of that one-inch-diameter stick to gyrate over water was a phenomenon that had to be seen to be believed. Some engineer somewhere must know of a meter that can be used to measure this tremendous energy, very nearly stronger than Richard Owen.

Richard offered me the stick. I took it and held it, but by

this time I had made up my mind that nothing was going to happen – and nothing did.

I asked Richard if he thought someone could be taught to find water or if possibly by practising ... but he didn't know. He had picked it up when he was nearly fifty. His boss on the farm had wanted to find a well or a spring on some lowland fields, too far out for the Water Board, so he had engaged a professional diviner. Richard had been seconded to act as diviner's mate for the afternoon – carry his hazel twigs and meters and things. During the afternoon the diviner had invited Richard to have a go and was amazed at the powerful reactions the twigs gave when he was holding them. Richard Owen regarded this water-divining as just another skill that a farm worker would find useful from time to time. I asked him if he was a medium. I knew before he answered that he wasn't. So I left the farm amazed at the demonstration of power I had witnessed, and yet very disappointed at not being able to do the thing myself.

Opposite the vicarage there is a small, wooded field. I thought I would go over and try with my hazel sticks just once more. I walked to the left of it and to the right of it. I walked up it and down it, and nothing, nothing happened. Emyr Hughes, the farmer, must have been watching me, and presently he turned up beside me on his tractor.

'You'll never find water with that rubbish,' he said, pointing at my hazel sticks. 'This is what you want to help you find water.'

He rummaged under the seat of his tractor and pulled out two lengths of heavy fencing wire. 'Come,' he said, 'I'll show you. You will find that your vicarage mains water runs at that end of the field. Let's see if we can find it.'

He walked slowly with his wires, like a two-gun-toting cowboy. He was holding the wires loosely and about nine inches away from his body. He walked for perhaps thirty feet, and slowly the wires in his hands crossed. He did it again and again, and every time the wires crossed in exactly the same spot. He then handed the wire to me.

'There you go,' he said. 'Hold them very loosely. Everyone can find water.'

I took the wires and held them very loosely about nine inches apart at shoulder level. When I came up to the water-main spot, the wires crossed. I took them into the main road and held them over a water gutter – and the wires crossed again. I ran to the vicarage with them and held them over our outside water tap – and the wires crossed. I knew from that moment that I was a water-diviner.

My wife and my son were at home, and I invited them both to my first public water-divining demonstration. They were very impressed and asked if they could have a go. For both of them, when the wires were held over water, they crossed violently.

For the next couple of days I asked everyone who visited the house to try my wires. The result of my controlled experiment was that out of thirteen people who held the wires, they crossed for twelve, and only remained static for one man. I must say I never was too partial to that particular man anyway.

I then reported back to my medium friends. I described to them my skill with the wires.

'Oh! Dowsing, you mean?' they said. 'We thought you were looking for a water-diviner.'

I had the distinct feeling that my mediumistic friends were looking down their noses at poor Richard Owen and his hazel twig companions.

'You stand over water – stick gyrates – and so what of it?' they said. 'There is water down below, but how far below and how many gallons a minute could one expect? The real dowser uses wires.'

I liked that, 'the real dowser' and 'using wires'. I was now in amongst the true prophets. The real dowser uses wires and by looking up tables or memorizing tables is able to estimate the depth of the water and its quantity.

One of the leading dowsers in North Wales was the Revd Father John Rudd who was, in his day, Roman Catholic priest at both Caernarfon and Bala. He had carried out valuable experiments in the art of dowsing, and they were both simple and convincing. He discovered, whilst idling away with his wires, that he had water pipes running underneath his dining-room floor. He held his wires over the spot in the dining-room and found that the wires crossed, leaving an angle of 120 degrees. He then nipped upstairs to the bedroom immediately above the dining-room and stood on the equivalent spot, and his wires crossed at an angle of 80 degrees. He then measured the distance between the dining-room floor and the bedroom floor, and he has the beginning of a formula. If wires held three feet from water (dining-room floor) give an angle of 120 degrees and wires held thirteen feet from water (bedroom floor) give an angle of 80 degrees how deep down would water be if it gave an angle of 45 degrees? Father Rudd was amongst the first to draw out tables for the less mathematically minded of us dowsers.

It appears, however, that the more mature dowsers no longer play around with water. Water-divining has been left to the farmer and his hazel twigs whilst the rest of us rely on the National Water Board. Good dowsers find other uses for their gift.

I found within hours of discovering my special gift that my wires would cross for me over water, and if I walked towards a blank wall, they would spring apart at an angle of 180 degrees. I immediately thought of the possibilities for blind people. If blind persons had two little antennae (wires) sticking out of a box, and these were connected to a bell or a buzzer, they could warn the blind person if he was walking into any solid object. Body radar would replace eyesight.

Father Rudd could also programme his wires to be sensitive to selected objects or chemicals, in very much the same way as dogs today are programmed to pick up the scent of drugs or explosives.

I did find it difficult at first to get used to the idea of programming a piece of wire to sniff anything out, but it is not the wire that sniffs and it is not the wire that is programmed to search and find, but the radar within the human operator himself. The wire is just an inanimate tool. If the human operator decides to seek for gold or alcohol or corn flakes, the wires have to obey.

Tom Jenkins, a wonderful dowser, demonstrated this to me. He gave me his car keys and said that if I hid them anywhere I liked in his big garden, he would find them in five minutes. I hid them in thick ivy that was growing on one of his apple trees, and I made doubly sure that Tom didn't even know which direction I had gone in his garden. It was a controlled experiment. When Tom started out from the house, his wire quivered and tugged or did something because he just walked up to the tree, put the wire near, to get a more detailed location, and then reached into the ivy to retrieve his keys.

There are also map dowsers. One such person (a churchwarden, so I believe him) told me how his son rang up from Manchester to say that his car had been stolen, that its documents were in the top drawer of his desk, and the police wanted them, so could he please post them. My informant tells me that, before he sent the car documents, he got hold of a large-scale map of Manchester, laid the documents on one corner of it and then held his wire antennae over the map. The wire moved in his hand and pointed to one spot only. He parcelled the car documents up for his son and put in a note, 'Tell the police to look for your car on the Altrincham Road, and around this map-reading point.' When the car was found, three weeks later, it had been abandoned on the Altrincham Road, but his mapping point was half a mile out.

It was only after reading Father Rudd's notes on his experiments that I began to understand why my Spiritualist friends always say, 'Everyone can heal' – 'Everyone has the gift of clairvoyance' – 'Everyone has the ability to divine water.' These sayings always used to annoy me, and I felt like saying to them, 'You speak for yourself, chum.' Now I think I understand. It is to do with the aura that is around all our bodies.

Do I hear someone say, 'Speak for yourself, chum. You are getting like your medium friends. There is no aura around my body'? There is, you know, and I can tell you how to find it.

All you have to do to find if you have an aura is to turn on your car radio and push down your aerial so that reception is weak; then get hold of your car aerial, and the radio volume will increase. This is because you are allowing your body to act as an aerial extension. Now do it all over again, only this time bring the palm of your hand slowly towards your weakened aerial but don't touch it. You will find that when your hand comes near to the aerial, the sound increases. It does not happen with me until I hold my palm about an inch away from the aerial. I suppose Winnie Marshall and Elwyn could activate the thing a good foot away.

The aura that enables us to do this is a kind of invisible

outer cover our bodies have. Those who know tell me that it is made of different layers, and the layers are different colours. I am not ashamed to confess that I don't know about these things. After all, I became a dowser only three days ago.

However, I didn't have to have the radio aerial experiment to convince me about the aura. I have very often seen Elwyn with a sort of thick halo around his whole body. It has nothing to do with his goodness. We all have the same aura. We are all at great pains to improve our intelligence and develop new skills with our minds, but we neglect the aura skills. This is why my friends say everyone can do wonderful things – they have the aura; all they have to do is use it.

Today I had to go back to the farm where my friend Richard Owen worked. I saw him at the other end of the field mending a fence, and I called out to him to say that I could divine water. The two of us then walked across the particular field that had lots of hidden springs, Richard Owen with his hazel twigs, me with my fence wires. I was so proud to be able to walk shoulder to shoulder with a real diviner of water. Every time Richard's hazel twig twisted, my wires would cross. Richard Owen took over my wires and held them far more tightly than I would have dared. The wires crossed every time for him. To end the demonstration, Richard held the wires and walked towards the cowshed wall.

'Let's see what signal they give here,' he said.

One yard away from the wall the wires opened out at 180 degrees to warn of the danger of walking into the wall. Richard Owen told me that there was also a pool of underground water at the same spot. The wire had a choice of two signals. Shout 'Water! Water!' or 'Look out! You're walking into a stone wall!' It very sensibly decided to give the warning.

There are also, I found, the pendulum people. They swing a small crystal pendulum to answer questions for them. These people are a breed apart. They always carry their pendulums in little leather cases close to their bodies, for the crystals are very often one-man crystals and can be temperamental. Some owners can come out with quite uncanny answers and results. Come Christmas, I may well equip myself with a crystal and a silk thread and a leather purse to keep it in.

6   Cis Jones

It is over forty years since the three gentlemen from the Spiritualist church over the fish shop in Bangor came to see me. One of them had said, 'Perhaps you would like to join us in a seance one evening, and then you will be better able to judge, brother,' and I had been terrified at the thought. And my old friend Ifan O. had counselled me not to go near 'that lot because they will wire the whole place up and frighten the pants off you'.

I did go near, and they didn't frighten me one little bit. These people who commune with the departed are such kind, friendly, gentle people, and I mean not only those who belong to the Spiritualist religion but also good Anglican and Methodist and no-denomination-at-all mediums. I have come to the conclusion that this gift is given to, or can be nurtured by, only the kind and the gentle. These people have strengthened my faith and enriched my ministry. Life after death is no longer something I hope for or believe in: I now know, without a shadow of doubt, that we will all leave our earthly bodies on this planet and continue our life in another spiritual existence.

What a pity the Bishop of Durham, as a young man and before he became the great scholar he is today, hadn't preached, as I did, against the evils of 'peeping beyond the veil' and the harm this can do to the 'weaker brethren'. He might then, perhaps, have had a visit from three elders of his local Spiritualist church and been invited to a seance and have been shown how to accept a mystery. Every Easter the poor Bishop, either in his own cathedral or in someone else's cathedral, seems to tarnish the joy of Easter for so many humble believers, and he sends the gentlemen of the media hurrying to telephone booths to send out headlines like 'Bishop Denies The Resurrection.'

Of course the Bishop does not deny the Resurrection. He believes firmly in the Resurrection. His message on Easter Day is the same as the message of all Christian people throughout the world: 'Christ is risen from the dead. Hallelujah.' But the Bishop of Durham is a great scholar, and he has the mind of a great scholar, and he feels unease at the thought of an empty grave. It is something he cannot logically explain. Jesus, to him, died on the Cross, and his body was buried in a grave on the first Good Friday. On Easter Day, and in a hot country, the Bishop would have expected the women to have witnessed a body that was beginning to putrefy and smell because the Risen Lord should by now have taken up his spiritual body. But the Gospels seem to glory in the fact that Christ never took on a spiritual body. He proudly exhibited his risen earthly body or a body that was continuous and yet discontinuous with his earthly body after the Resurrection. He broke bread with the disciples in Emmaus; he invited Thomas to touch his crucifixion scars; he breakfasted on fish and bread with his disciples on the beach, The Bishop's logical mind refuses to accept this idea of an earthly eating and breathing body sustaining itself in Paradise. To him and to other Christians, 'Christ is the first fruit of them that rise from the dead.'

Why then did God make his resurrection so different from the resurrection of the rest of us? We all cast away our earthly body – it is burned in an incinerator or buried deeply in the ground or cast into the depth of the sea, and we then take on a look-alike spiritual body that is free of earthly limitations.

I am sure the Bishop of Durham would be quite unimpressed if he ever came to find out that Aelwyn Roberts, vicar of Llandegai in the diocese of Bangor, feels just as unhappy and as ill at ease at the story of the empty grave as he does. There must be times in the lives of us all when we feel that, if we were God and had the power of the godhead, we would have ordered things a little differently from, and perhaps a little more logically than, the Almighty himself. For me, this is one of those times. I think I would have allowed the women to enter the grave and embalm the body of Jesus, and allowed the men to come later and seal the grave, as was the custom. Then, on the Resurrection Day, the faithful would see again their Lord and Master, but see Him in his new spiritual body. I think the Bishop of Durham would like that kind of resurrection too.

For a long time the Protestant Church has turned a deaf ear to the resurrection as described by St Paul (and let us not forget that he, like the disciples, had seen the Risen Lord). St Paul says quite clearly,

> But some men will say, 'How are the dead raised up and with what body do they come?' Thou fool, that which thou sowest is not quickened except it die ...
>
> There are celestial bodies and bodies terrestrial but the glory of the celestial is one and the glory of the terrestrial is another ... so also is the resurrection of the dead. It is sown in corruption; it is raised in incorruption ... it is sown a natural body; it is raised a spiritual body. There is a natural body and there is a spiritual body. (I Corinthians 15.)

Although the church places this great scholarly treatise on the Resurrection as the lesson to be read at funeral services in the Anglican Church, it has always reverted, very quietly, after the funeral to its preferred theology of the empty grave of the Gospels.

The Bishop of Durham and the vicar of Llandegai have been brought up to recite every Sunday the Creeds that we share with our brethren of the Roman Catholic Church, the Apostles' Creed at Matins and Evensong: 'I believe in God the Father Almighty ... in Jesus Christ ... in the Holy Spirit ... and in the resurrection of the body.' On special occasions we recite the Athanasian Creed: 'The Catholic faith is this that we shall worship one God in Trinity and the Trinity in Unity ... and [we believe that at Christ's] coming all men shall rise again with their bodies.'

The Bishop of Durham and the vicar of Llandegai both remember singing Hymn 575 in *Hymns Ancient and Modern*:

> Within the churchyard, side by side,
>   Are many long low graves;
> And some have stones set over them,
>   On some the green grass waves.
>
> Full many a little Christian child,
>   Woman, and man, lies there;

And we pass near them every time
   When we go in to prayer.

They do not hear when the great bell
   Is ringing overhead:
They cannot rise and come to Church
   With us, for they are dead.

But we believe a day shall come
   When all the dead will rise,
When they who sleep down in the grave
   Will ope again their eyes.

For Christ our Lord was buried once,
   He died and rose again,
He conque'd death, He left the grave;
   And so will Christian men

                        Mrs Alexander

In the slate quarry town of Blaenau Ffestiniog, where I was brought up, if a man lost a leg or an arm, or even a finger, in a quarry accident, the cut-off limb would be carefully placed in a little casket and buried in a place apart, in the churchyard, and its place would be marked in the church register. Years later, when Richard Jones or William Davies died of old age his body was laid to rest where the missing limb awaited him. In this way Richard Jones or William Davies could arise whole on the Resurrection Day. I don't think anyone ever taught openly the doctrine of the resurrection of the body, but there was a reluctance to tell the layman, in the pew, that after death the earthly body would be discarded.

So, like the Bishop of Durham, but years ahead of him, I decided to tell, to leak information about the temporary status of the earthly body. I didn't, however, shout it out into the microphones of the media and the pages of the *News of the World*. I tried it out tentatively on my second congregation. I have two congregations in Llandegai. I have the regulars who come to Communion and to Matins on Sunday, and I have the gypsies who come to baptisms, marriages and burials. My gypsy parishioners are very religious people. Ecumenically they are a model to others. They sit down with heads cupped in their right hand for prayers, as the Evangelicals do, and at the end of prayers they make the sign of the cross, as the Romans do. They call me their Protestant Father, and word has gone round the camp that, if you want your caravan blessed, you should ask the Protestant Father, because he uses far more holy water than the Roman father. This pleases me.

The gypsies have a firm grasp of the doctrine of the Anglican Church, and it is passed on from mother to child, but it is a good fifty years behind the times. When I arrange gypsy funerals, I realize that my gypsy parishioners believe today what the ordinary Anglican believed fifty years ago. The gypsies believe in the resurrection of the body, no question about it. They have never heard of the Bishop of Durham or his theology. (The gypsies of AD 2040 might come to know of him.) To them, death and the afterlife are a great, great mystery. They are scared of death. They are in panic when it strikes the camp. They bury their dead in expensive caskets (bury, not cremate); the graves are lined with flower-decorated silks and satins. They gather from miles and miles to attend funerals, and special lorries carry the thousands and thousands of pounds' worth of floral tributes. Massive marble memorials are then built over the graves. Expensive sacrifices to the great unknown.

Some years ago I buried the wonderful old gypsy lady who had been queen of our village settlement. Her six sons, bedecked in black suits and ties, squashed themselves uncomfortably into the front pew and cried loudly and unashamedly. I never normally say much at funerals, but on this day, with my little church packed and smitten with grief and doubts and fears, I decided to teach the faith to my less learned parishioners.

I walked up to the coffin, laid my hands on it and told them, 'Jemimah Ruth is not in this coffin. It is only her earthly body that is here. She has no need of this body any more, so she is asking her sons to get rid of it. She wants them to place it in a deep hole in the ground and shovel soil on it and to do this quickly before it begins to rot. Jemimah has now a new body, a spiritual body ...'

I could see my gypsy friends recoiling from me, looking down at the floor, shuffling their feet. The Protestant Father whom they had all trusted was now teaching something they did not understand or like. I realized my mistake. It had taken my other congregation from the questions that followed the Great War of 1914–18 to the consecration of the Bishop of Durham to wrestle with this problem that I was asking my poor gypsies to resolve in one afternoon. It must be added that in the days after the funeral the six brothers came to the vicarage at night: they wanted to know, in the privacy of my study, a little more about their mother's new spiritual body.

In the Great War, thousands of young men were shelled and bombed, and their bodies were blown to smithereens. Questions were asked. The family who buried William Davies' arm in the churchyard in Blaenau Ffestiniog wanted to know who would gather up and bury all the little bits of his son's body blown up in Ypres. If this could not be done, what would become of the heroes of Mons and Ypres and Gallipoli on the Resurrection Day? The Church took fright, and the Lambeth Conference of 1920 set up a commission of two archbishops and thirty bishops to seek an answer from the Spiritualists. In 1938 Archbishop Lang set up his own commission into the faith of the Spiritualists and went and locked it away for many years. I often wonder if he suffered pangs of conscience as leader of the whole Anglican Church when he came to make arrangements for his own funeral in 1945. Whatever the reason, it was found that the Archbishop had requested that at death his body was to be cremated. Many of the great theologians of his day declared that, by asking for his body to be burned, the Archbishop had preached a far more powerful sermon in death than he had ever preached in life.

The Church does move. The Holy Spirit does reveal new truths about God to every generation. Every age has its own prophets. But if I could be God for just one more time, I think I would chose a different prophet for the 1980s. Prophet Jenkins of Durham is not a very good communicator.

After having dealings with the Spiritualists and knowing mediums who have opened doors for me to peep through into the afterlife, I am constantly mystified. I cannot begin to explain to myself why a little family living in a country vicarage, close to mine, are terrified of visits from a huge, dirty old goat that appears about three or four times a year in their sitting-room; it glowers at them for minutes on end and then disappears. My medium friends talk of ectoplasm and other things, but they have no idea either. They are equally mystified.

It puzzles me why the departed, when they appear to us on earth, dress their spiritual bodies in the clothes of the period of their death. I do admit that it is, perhaps, more respectable and more seemly to communicate with clothed ghosts than with spiritual streakers, but I still think the gold watch and chain are an unnecessary appendage, and it worries me. Animal ghosts, anniversary ghosts, earthbound ghosts and ghosts with an eighteen-carat watch and chain are all mysteries to me. Under the influence of mediums one learns to accept mysteries. Mediumship teaches great patience in the presence of mystification.

So the empty grave becomes one more mystery. The only explanation that I offer to myself is that perhaps the disciples, after witnessing the horrible death of their Master, needed that kind of earthly manifestation at that time, and that God, knowing how they were soon to be scattered and separated and persecuted, allowed them this special kind of manifestation. I can, and I do, accept this as the Miracle of the Resurrection. It is so true that both the vicar of Llandegai and the Bishop of Durham '... now see through a glass darkly but then face to face'. I can wait.

Today I was arranging the funeral of a young friend who had died of cancer aged forty-seven. During the last two weeks of a very short illness she had attended Spiritualist healing services. She had received a great deal of courage, inner calm and serenity from the laying-on of hands at these services. Her husband asked me if it would be possible to allow her Spiritualist healer to say a few words at the crematorium service.

I hesitated for perhaps three seconds, sufficient time for her poor husband to say to me, 'Not if it means getting you into trouble, vicar.'

I was trying to remember very quickly if Spiritualists were heretics or something, and whether it was a matter that had to be cleared with my bishop. I decided that it couldn't possibly be an unfrockable matter, and I told my friend, 'Yes, do please ask your medium friend to say a few words.'

St Paul describes the first-century Church in words that an

MP quoted in the House of Commons when they were debating the repeal of the Witchcraft Act: 'Now concerning spiritual gifts, brethren. I would not have you ignorant,' and he goes on to say, 'The manifestation of the spirit is given to every man to profit withal. For to one is given ... the gift of healing by the same spirit. To another the working of miracles, to another prophecy, and to another the discerning of spirits.' (I Cor. 12.)

After reading these words I felt there must be something very wrong with me, or with my Church, or with my bishop, or with the whole lot of us, for me to have to hesitate for the whole of three seconds before deciding there was nothing ecclesiastically wrong in my inviting a Christian Spiritualist to take part in an Anglican funeral at a crematorium, and to have to ask myself whether or not these kind, loving, Christian people I had met were heretics or schismatics or some other kind of 'ics'. Then the thought occurred to me that, if they were really good, bona fide Christians, how they could enrich the life of the great old mother Church. They could teach us how to regain and re-use the gift of 'healing' and the gift of 'discerning spirits' that we once received and seem to have lost.

I had a dream. I was a minor canon at Bangor Cathedral once again, and I was reading the announcements.

'The cathedral services next Sunday will be as follows:

'Holy Communion at 8 a.m.

'Choral Communion at 11.15. The preacher will be the Very Reverend the Dean.

'The evening service will be held in the crypt at 6.30 p.m. The medium for this evening's service will be Mrs Winnie Marshall of Colwyn Bay. Members are asked to bring flowers so that the medium can deliver messages.

'A service of spiritualist healing will follow.'

And the Evangelicals shouted 'Hallelujah,' and the Romans 'Hail, Mary, full of grace,' and the great old Church of England marched across the threshold of a new century, enriched and endowed with reconditioned spiritual gifts, and the brave little Spiritualist Church gained by receiving the discipline of a new mother Church through her creeds and her traditions.

*

I have already said that my own ministry was enriched through my new knowledge of the beyond. Cis Jones told me this on her death-bed many years ago.

Cis Jones was a very faithful, though very peculiar, parishioner. Other parishioners called her Miss Jones, and 'Cis' behind her back. She was a recluse. She lived frugally in a small terraced house in the village but was reputed to be very rich. She attended church regularly, morning and evening, and was among the last to enter and the first to leave. She was always dressed in black, and winter and summer she wrapped a black chiffon scarf round the lower part of her face.

When I called on my pastoral visitations, Miss Jones and I always had plenty to talk about. The recluse, in her own house, was a very charming person. I gathered that in younger days Miss Jones had been a bit of a daredevil. In 1928 she used to ride a Norton 500. She was also a great swimmer. In those days when people were only just beginning to discover the enjoyment of the sea, and when even the bravest males donned voluminous bathing-costumes, in the privacy of a bathing-hut, Cis would undress quietly on a lonely beach and swim for miles into the empty sea. There had been an engagement, or at least some tacit understanding, between her and a young curate, but it had come to nothing, and people said that Miss Jones had become peculiar because she had been 'disappointed in love'.

She must have been in her seventies when she was rushed to hospital. There were the usual tests and an exploratory operation, and at the end Miss Jones made them tell all. They told her she had but weeks to live – at most three months. She discharged herself from hospital and came back to her own home. She told me what they had told her in hospital and that she wanted to make her will.

Many of her neighbours had told me they would like to help. But they didn't like to call and offer because '– well, you know what Cis is like.' I passed the message to Miss Jones, and she considered it.

'I'll have to pay them, I suppose.'

'Don't you dare insult them with your money!' I told her.

Miss Jones lived for ten weeks after we had drawn up a rota of neighbour help. I don't know how happy she had

been as a young lady, riding her Norton and swimming to
far-off beaches, but I do know she had the time of her life
during her last ten weeks. Neighbours were in and out,
whether it was their duty time or not. Cis was the life of the
party. She had found love, friendliness and good fellowship.
She had attended church all her life, but it was only in these
last ten weeks that she found what it was all about.

She was in pain, in great pain, but she tried not to show it.
Her doctor came to see me.

'I wonder,' he said, 'if you could persuade Miss Jones to
take medication for her pain.'

He explained to me that she was physically strong and, for
this reason, up to now he had not offered pain-killing drugs
but was reserving them for the final stages. When, however,
he considered the time had come to start on a graduated
course of morphine, Miss Jones had refused to have anything
to do with pain-killers. She had told him she wouldn't even
take an aspirin.

When I went to see her the next day, I told her about the
doctor's concern and asked why she objected so much to
taking pain-killers.

'I'm surprised at you of all people asking me that,' she
replied. 'Don't you remember how, last Easter, you preached
about the Resurrection and in your sermon you said that
when a person died he would close his eyes and ears to this
world and open them in another. And then,' she said, 'you
went on to quote from a book that had been written by some
doctor. You said that this doctor had interviewed many
people who had died and who had been resuscitated, and
how they all described what they had seen; how they had
heard wonderful music; how they had walked through some
tunnel where they felt so happy; and how they had seen their
parents beckoning to them and welcoming them.'

'Yes,' I said, 'I did say all that, and I believe it to be the
truth.'

'Well then,' said Cis, 'how is it that you now ask me such a
stupid question as why I refuse to take morphia? I don't want
to be doped and muddle-headed when this exciting thing
happens to me! I want to enjoy my death when it comes!'

7 Elwyn's Glossary

Author's Note. I do feel that having come to the end of my story, some readers might like a more detailed description of some of the terms used. My good friend and companion has very kindly consented to write the Glossary and who better suited for the task than Elwyn Roberts, Wales's Crowned Bard, research scientist, member of the National Association of Hypnotists and Psychotherapists and associate member of the Society for Psychical Research.

OBE – Out of Body Experience (See 'The Ghost of a Living Man').

It has been known for many centuries that it is possible, under certain circumstances, for the centre of consciousness to leave the body so that the person then observes the world from a position other than where the body is.

OBE can happen spontaneously when a person is totally relaxed or in a state between sleep and awakeness. Others have experienced this sensation at the time of an accident or in a Near Death Experience. There are some who claim to be able to bring about this condition at will, through meditation, visualization and other methods. The effect can also be induced in some hypnotized persons.

In many spontaneous OBEs, the displaced consciousness remains close to the body, in the same room as the body and often at an elevated position. It is not uncommon for seriously ill hospital patients to observe the whole resuscitation attempt being carried out on their bodies by medical staff.

There is not a great deal written about long-distance projection of the centre of consciousness, but a tale is told by a young man who had been in an accident of how he managed to project himself back to his own home only to be totally ignored by members of his family, who could apparently neither see nor hear him. The only reaction to his homecoming was from his dog, which wagged its tail profusely at him.

During my own OBE I always felt that I was outside, and completely independent of, my own body. I could move my centre of consciousness at will to any part of the room and even stand behind my own body. I am sure I retained my normal senses, and I was capable of thought and decision. I was afraid of going too far from my body, and returning to it was always my own conscious decision. All my OBEs were spontaneous: as a child it was before going to sleep; as an adult it has been whilst sitting in a psychic circle.

It has always been my ambition to break out of the body at will and to extend its travel. Is death that state in which the centre of consciousness is permanently cut off from the physical body? Many who believe this and have themselves experienced OBEs in life have no fear of death.

Many Spiritualists, and others, believe that we carry the spiritual body within the earthly frame and that during OBE it is the spiritual body that is looking down on the earthly. In death could it be that the chrysalis is left for burial whilst the butterfly has already flown.

Mediumship

This term belongs to the Spiritualists. They believe that a medium can bridge the gap between the spiritual and the physical worlds. There are various forms of mediumship. The most common is the kind where the medium is able to receive images and sounds and feelings of others around him. Sometimes a medium can give surprisingly accurate descriptions of people (often dead) and of places and events connected with them. They also seem to pass messages between spiritual beings and their earthly relatives and friends.

Some mediums in trance appear to lend their bodies temporarily to a spiritual entity, so that it can communicate directly with earth-dwellers.

Another interesting form of mediumship is transfiguration. In this case it might be possible for observers to see a misty substance collect around a medium and form itself into the recognizable shape of another person (often dead). The effects are better seen at low lighting levels, when the eye is most sensitive. Mediums who are able to transfigurate simultaneously act as mental or trans mediums, so that verbal as well as pictorial contacts can be made. The picture usually forms upon the medium, but occasionally to one side.

It is claimed that there are, or have been, physical mediums who in some way allow spiritual entities to manifest themselves in physical form. In the past many of these were exposed as frauds, but there is strong evidence that some were genuine. The lifting of objects (including the medium!) and other psychokinetic (PK) actions have been reported and recorded.

The Spiritualist belief is that mediums do act as interfaces with the dead. (Presumably 'dead' is an incorrect term for any 'being' that is able to communicate.) There could, however, be other explanations. Some examples of mental mediumship could be explained as a form of telepathy between medium and recipient, at an unconscious level. The PK phenomenon does not necessarily come about by spirit intervention. Our own human minds it appears can directly affect matter. Certainly poltergeist activity does often exhibit very humanlike traits of spontaneity, cunningness and apparent emotions, such as shyness and anger.

Parapsychology

Parapsychology is the study of the mental capabilities beyond the five accepted senses. It includes the study of mediumship, clairvoyance, telepathy, PK, poltergeist, OBEs and the possible survival of the mind after death. Man's knowledge of his own mental and physical make-up has broken all barriers over the past fifty years. There are many who believe that we are on the brink of great discoveries about man's spiritual make-up and his aura in the years to come.

Aura

The aura is a sort of halo that according to some people surrounds our bodies. It is a subject of great speculation. Many Spiritualist healers maintain that they can diagnose illness more effectively by observing the aura of a patient rather than the physical symptoms.

Kirlian Photography

This is the discovery, by two Russian scientists, of the means of taking photographs of auras in a radio frequency field. Through this it has been discovered that not only humans but also animals and vegetation carry their own aura. When a person or an animal or a vegetable dies, the aura is extinguished. Cameras played on the hands of humans have shown that, as their moods change, so do the brightness and the intensity of their body aura. If, as some Spiritualist healers say, sickness symptoms appear first in the aura, before becoming visibly present in the body, Kirlian photography could play an exciting part in future medical diagnosis.

The Society for Psychical Research

For more than a hundred years this society, led by eminent scholars, has been investigating reports of paranormal activity and reporting its findings in a scientific manner. Important discoveries have been made. The work is continuing.

The purpose is to solve the greatest mystery of all: does the mind emanate from matter or is it an entity of itself that merely uses matter to express itself? If the former, when matter dies, the whole person dies: death extinguishes all. If the latter, there has to be after death a world of 'minds' (spirits) of which we *all* are a part now, and *all*, in this context, must include those who still retain their physical bodies together with those whose physical bodies have long perished.